THE WESTERN FRONT
1914–1918

*

Correlli Barnett, *Yorkshire Post*

'This collection of essays is really about the British and the Western Front . . . John Terraine's nine essays either help our understanding or stimulate our thought.'

Sir Charles Petrie, *Illustrated London News*

'Mr. Terraine has made the First World War very much his own, to the great advantage of all students of it . . . Now we have a collection of penetrating essays on the conflict as a whole, and there can be no higher praise than to say they are up to the standard which his previous work has led us to expect.'

The Times

'Mr. John Terraine reflects with insight and compassion on the appalling shambles of the Western Front.'

Also in Arrow Books by John Terraine
The Great War

John Terraine

The Western Front
1914–1918

ARROW BOOKS

ARROW BOOKS LTD
178–202 Great Portland Street, London W1

 AN IMPRINT OF THE HUTCHINSON GROUP

London Melbourne Sydney
Auckland Bombay Toronto
Johannesburg New York

✳

First published by
Hutchinson & Co (*Publishers*) Ltd June 1964
Reprinted before publication
Third impression November 1965
Fourth impression August 1967
Arrow edition January 1970

*Made and printed in Great Britain
by The Anchor Press Ltd.,
Tiptree, Essex*
09 002610 1

To those who were less fortunate than myself;
who were born in time to serve on the Western Front.

Acknowledgements

Acknowledgements are due to the Editors of *History Today* for permission to reprint 'Armistice 1918' (November 1958), 'The Genesis of the Western Front' (July 1960), 'Lloyd George's Dilemma' (May 1961), 'Lloyd George's Expedients' (April and May 1963), 'The Battle of Guise' (February 1960) and 'Big Battalions: The Napoleonic Legacy' (June 1962); to the Editor of the *Journal of the Royal United Service Institution* for permission to reprint 'Passchendaele and Amiens' (May and August 1959) and 'Haig: 1861–1928' (November 1961); and to the Editor of *The Spectator* for permission to reprint 'A Soldier's Soldier' (June 1957).

My thanks are due to authors and publishers who have given permission for quotations from the following books: *A Subaltern's War* by Charles Edmonds, published by Peter Davies Ltd.; *Haldane: An Autobiography*, published by Hodder & Stoughton Ltd.; *The World Crisis* by Winston S. Churchill, published by Odhams Books Ltd.; *Soldiers and Statesmen 1914–1918* by Field-Marshal Sir William Robertson, published by Cassell & Co. Ltd.; and *Men and Power* by Lord Beaverbrook, published by Hutchinson & Co. (Publishers) Ltd.

Contents

Illustrations

PLATES

MAPS

Acknowledgements are due to those who have
provided and given permission for the use of illus-
trative material in this book: Radio Times Hulton
Picture Library for numbers 2, 4, 7, 11, and 16;
Paul Popper Ltd. for numbers 5, 6 and 18; the
Imperial War Museum for numbers 1, 3, 8, 10, 13,
14, 15, 17, and 19; and *History Today* for number 12
and maps of the battles of Guise and Amiens.

INTRODUCTION

The Western Front, 1914-1918, was a unique phenomenon. It was also, for the nations whose armies were
devoured by it, a shocking phenomenon. This shock
was produced by the great losses which the armies sustained, both cumulatively and incident by incident,
apparently for little purpose. A great sense of waste
was thus engendered, and this was almost wholly due
to the exceptional quality of the Western Front itself :
its grotesquely static nature.

The losses themselves were not exceptional. They
were probably exceeded, even at the time, by those on
the less publicised Eastern Front, where Russia alone
is said to have lost two million men in 1915, and a
million more in 1916, and where the Habsburg Empire
met its doom. During the Second World War the
Eastern Front witnessed even more dreadful scenes
and greater bloodbaths; the Soviet Union revealed, in
its post-war census returns, a loss of twenty million
people between 1941 and 1945, 10 per cent of her
total population. These considerations, of course, were
beyond the knowledge of the 1914-1918 generation;
laymen and politicians understandably quailed at what
seemed to be an unexampled evil. The scale of events
was, indeed, unexampled; their character was not.
Those who had studied military history (an unfashion-
able pursuit) could point to many occasions when a

similar balance of force had produced similar dire results. They could add that the growing human and
material resources of modern states had already visibly
multiplied the cost of war, and might be expected to
go on doing so.

It was, above all, the entry of the masses into war
that produced the most fearsome slaughters; this was
a process which began in Europe with the French
Revolution. During the Napoleonic period, all the important European nations except England became
familiar with the sanguinary and destructive tendency
of the new warfare. One of the essays in this book will
point out the folly of supposing that Napoleon possessed some 'answer' to this problem; on the contrary he
was one of its principal originators. His last battle,
Waterloo, illustrates the case : according to the latest
researches, the cost of Waterloo was 10,813 dead and
36,195 wounded,[1] a total of just under 47,000 out of
some 150,000 engaged. This is roughly the same proportion of 30 per cent of the overall British losses on
that fatal and notorious day, July 1st 1916, of the
First Battle of the Somme, when the British Army lost
57,000 men.

Overall percentages, of course, conceal terrible individual statistics : on the Somme, on July 1st, the 1st
Newfoundland Regiment lost 710 officers and men,
and was 'literally annihilated';[2] in the same division,
the 2nd Royal Fusiliers had 561 casualties, the 16th
Middlesex 549, the 1st K.O.S.B. 552, the 1st Inniskil-
ling Fusiliers 568, and the 1st Border Regiment 575,
all these constituting percentages of well over 60. The
16th Royal Scots (34th Division) had the melancholy

distinction of 333 dead out of 466 who fell—a most unusual and dreadful proportion.

Waterloo tells a similar tale. There, it was the defeated French who contributed most to the carnage; but there were grim losses among some of the British regiments. The 1st Dragoon Guards lost 246 out of 571; the 6th Dragoons, 217 out of 445; the 3rd Battalion 1st Foot Guards, 342 out of 860; the 30th Foot, 228 out of 635; the 73rd Foot, 280 out of 498; the 1st Battalion 95th Rifles, 156 out of 418, and the 2nd Battalion of that regiment, 246 out of 655. The British total of 7,000 out of 24,000 engaged once again approaches closely the 30 per cent which seems to be the minimum that evenly balanced modern battle exacts.

If, after Waterloo, there was time for the Western European nations to forget this lesson it was duly repeated in the Crimea. But the most salutary warning came from America, where an industrial society, making full use of the most up-to-date power-source—steam—revealed what follows the mobilisation of nations so equipped. The American Civil War (1861-1865) ended with a million dead; within that figure were contained battles of extraordinary bloodiness: '. . . 115 regiments—63 Union and 52 Confederate —sustained losses of more than 50 per cent in a single engagement. At Antietam 82.3 per cent of the officers and men of the First Texas Regiment were killed or wounded. At Gettysburg the First Minnosota Regiment lost 82 per cent. . . .'

Yet, alarming though these figures were, they did not express the full danger that lay ahead. That was revealed in a time comparison; for at Waterloo nine hours contained the whole butchery, and three days' fighting sufficed to overthrow Napoleon; the North took four years to defeat the outwardly much weaker and less industrialised South. Evidently, a balance of force had somehow been struck, and the effect of such a balance was to be seen in the grim casualty lists of the war. In 1914 a similar balance was arrived at, and the results were the same; only now it was not one nation divided against itself that fought, but the whole concourse of 'civilised' powers.

Casualties — even very great casualties — can be made bearable if they are accompanied by striking achievements, best of all if they lead to swift and decisive results. On the Western Front, between 1914 and 1918, nothing of that kind seemed to be happening. Instead, at a human cost which mounted steadily as the armies grew to their unprecedented hugeness, only the most seemingly insignificant gains of ground were made, and decisive results constantly failed to reward even the most ferocious struggles.

The Second Battle of Champagne, the culminating offensive by which the French hoped to expel the Germans from their soil in 1915, produced 145,000 French casualties—and a gain that was nowhere deeper than 3,000 yards. The Battle of Verdun swayed to and fro for nearly ten months of 1916, costing the French and Germans between them about three-quarters of a million casualties, and at the end of it the front was almost exactly where it had been when the whole thing started. The Battle of the Somme, in the same year, cost the British Army 415,000 casualties in four and a half months, and when it closed under the onset of a pitiless winter ground objectives laid down for the first day were still unattained. In 1917 the Third Battle of Ypres (Passchendaele) cost the British about a quarter of a million men in three and a half months, and their furthest advance was some seven miles. Not until 1918 was any appreciable movement felt on the Western Front.

By contrast on the Russian front, forward and backward movements of up to 300 miles were common; coloured pins leapt about on the maps of armchair strategists. It escaped notice that sensational manœuvres, whether in the West or in the East, tended to be fruitless. What counted, in both areas, was the battles. Movement was its reward—or penalty. And it was in the West that the ultimate rewards and penalties were seen.

While they were being awaited, however, the grimness of the style of war, the brutality of the 'slogging match', the squalor and weariness of 'trench warfare', had a searing effect upon the human spirit. This was true of all armies and peoples, but more particularly so of the Allies. The Germans, after all, were fighting on conquered soil; the French, on the other hand, found themselves gripped by the horrible necessity of destroying their own land and its resources. A large part of their country was in enemy hands; another large part formed the 'zone of the armies', a state within a state, a place to which men went in thousands, and never came back, or returned hideously mutilated in body or mind.

The British, too, just across the Channel, had the

frightening sense of their manhood being sucked into this all-too-familiar vortex. Soldiers manned the same trenches for months—sometimes years—on end; took their spells out of the line, and returned to the same dug-outs, the same saps, the same corpses, the same smells and dirt; they went on leave to England (which seemed like another planet where no one spoke their language) and came back again to the old billet, the old mud, the old shelling and the old comrades, with a few more faces missing since they went away. There was an inexpressible tedium and frustration about it all, between the terrors of the great battles, partly conveyed in the constant repetition of intrinsically uninteresting place-names—dreary Etaples, the B.E.F.'s base camp; Poperinghe, the last 'staging-point' on the way to shattered Ypres; Armentières, famous in song; Bethune, facing the unappetising, waterlogged, industrial lowlands of La Bassée; Loos and Lens; Albert on the Somme, with its legendary 'hanging virgin' looking down with compassion on the endless parade below.

All this would have been unendurable but for the inexhaustible patience and cheerfulness of the troops. Even at the time these qualities largely cut them off from communication with their relatives at home, whose views and sentiments, fed upon misleading communiqués and absurd Press propaganda, swung from wild optimism to gloomy disillusionment as the years went by. Lord Douglas of Kirtleside, who went out to France in November 1914 with the Royal Horse Artillery, has written : 'There was no such thing as public relations because officialdom thought it best that the public should remain in stupefied ignorance.'[4] As time

passed, the dangers of this policy—if policy it was—
became acute. 'England was beastly in 1918', wrote
one officer. 'It was in the hands of the dismal and in-
competent. Pessimism raged among those who knew
nothing of the war. . . . Only in the trenches (on both
sides of No Man's Land) were chivalry and sweet rea-
sonableness to be found.'[5] The same man also wrote:

'A legend has grown up, propagated not by
soldiers but by journalists, that these men who went
gaily to fight in the mood of Rupert Brooke and
Julian Grenfell, lost their faith amid the horrors of
the trenches and returned in a mood of anger and
despair. To calculate the effect of mental and bodily
suffering, not on a man but on a whole generation
of men, may seem an impossible task, but at least it
can be affirmed that the legend of disenchantment
is false.'

Those words appeared in 1929, the period of the
Slump and the great Depression. In 1933 another regimental officer wrote: '. . . this post-war propaganda,
piling corpse on corpse, heaping horror on futility,
seems bound to fail from every point of view. In its
distortion, the soldier looks in vain for the scenes he
knew.'[6] Already, when these views appeared, they
were challenging; today they seem almost unbelievable.
It is almost impossible to recapture the frame of mind
of the generation of fifty years ago. 'The modern intellectual is inclined to look with impatience upon the
ardour with which they went to war. Looking back,
the intensity—and I dare add the purity—of that
spirit still moves me deeply,' writes Captain Cyril

Falls. To the extent that one can recapture this feeling it becomes unutterably poignant. It is a phenomenon requiring the utmost effort of comprehension; it deserves more than dismissal with the cruel verdict, 'futile waste'.

These essays, written over a period of years, mark stages in my own attempt to understand what was happening on the Western Front, where our fathers and grandfathers spent their lives so freely. In editing them for publication I have altered very little. Here and there I have tried to clarify a badly expressed thought; where I have noticed factual inaccuracies I have corrected them. But I have left the arguments intact, as they first appeared in print, preferring to explain my altered viewpoint in a note at the end of the essay.

It may seem odd to begin at the end, with the Armistice of 1918; but it is not strange really. On the contrary, it is appropriate to start by counting the cost of an experience which has left its mark on all the later years.

NOTES

1. Article, 'Le Charnier de Waterloo' by Leo Fleischman, in *L'histoire Pour Tous*, June 1961.

2. Official History.

3. Bell Irvin Wiley : *They Who Fought Here*. New York : Macmillan 1959.

4. *Years of Combat*. London : Collins, 1963.

5. Charles Edmonds : *A Subaltern's War*. London : Peter Davies, 1929.

6. Sidney Rogerson : *Twelve Days*. London : Arthur Barker, 1933.

ARMISTICE
1918

When the guns ceased firing at 11 a.m. on November 11th, 1918, and the war ended at last, the land forces of the British Empire numbered over four and three-quarter million combatant troops. Of this total, more than three and half million were from the United Kingdom. The size of these figures constitutes the most significant fact about the First World War from the British point of view. The rejoicing and happiness of Armistice Day, as of V.E. Day and V.J. Day twenty-seven years later, were spontaneous and natural. But both in 1918 and in 1945 they were compounded mainly of relief at the ending of dreadful ordeal, and pride at the fortitude with which it had been borne. For Britain, on each occasion, the victory lay in what had been averted, not in what had been achieved. Each struggle contributed a stage in the contraction of British power, in the diminution of Britain's status in the world. The origin of that transformation lies in the manner in which she fought the First World War.

The year 1918 witnessed the nadir and the zenith of the British Army's effort. When it opened there were approximately two million British troops in France and Flanders, of whom half were combatants. The infantry were organised in fifty-seven divisions, forty-seven of them from the United Kingdom. In

March the Germans began the series of offensives by which they hoped to win swift victory : the British Army was their principal target. They succeeded in driving back and largely destroying the Fifth Army in Picardy, but they failed to break the Allied front. When this attack stopped on April 5th the British had suffered 163,943 casualties. On April 9th the Germans launched a new attack on the Ypres–Armentières front, where an advance to only half the distance covered in Picardy would have brought them to the Channel. Two days later Field-Marshal Sir Douglas Haig issued the famous Order of the Day which ended with these words.

'There must be no retirement. With our backs to the wall and believing in the justice of our cause each one must fight on to the end. The safety of our homes and the freedom of mankind alike depend upon the conduct of each one of us at this critical moment.'

The German attack was held; but by April 21st, when the purely defensive fighting on the British front ended, casualties had risen to almost 250,000, as many as those at Passchendaele, almost all of them infantry. The British Army appeared to be at its last gasp. Yet within a matter of weeks it had embarked upon one of its greatest victories.

Despite the weakness of his Army, and the paucity of the reinforcements he received, Haig was quick to grasp a possibility of victory after the failure of the two huge German blows. As early as January 7th, 1918, the Intelligence Branch of G.H.Q. had stated that

'The German accession of morale is not of a permanent character and is not likely to stand the strain of
an unsuccessful attack with consequent losses. . . . If
Germany attacks and fails she will be ruined.' It was
on this conclusion, contrary to the prevailing pessimism
of the period, that Haig based his ideas. New and
massive German onslaughts were still to be delivered
against the French in May, June and July. These again
achieved spectacular successes, but failed in their main
object. And, already at Villers Bretonneux, on April
25th, British troops had counter-attacked on a local
scale. On May 17th Haig had instructed plans to be
drawn up for a large offensive in the Amiens area. The
prelude of this was the Battle of Le Hamel on July
4th; and the great attack itself was delivered by the
British Fourth Army on August 8th, the 'black day' of
the German Army. From then until the Armistice on
November 11th the British Army advanced continuously, breaking the Hindenburg Line, and driving the
enemy back to the area of the first battlefields of 1914.
In four months of ceaseless attack it captured 188,700
prisoners and 2,840 guns; the French, Americans and
Belgians in the same period captured between them
196,500 prisoners and 3,775 guns. The British achievement was superb, but the cost of it went far beyond
the 350,000 casualties sustained in this grand victorious
offensive.

These are the bald facts. Like most of the statistics
of the First World War they have a stupefying quality.
It is impossible to visualise 350,000 casualties. It is only
by an intense effort that one can visualise the arena
and the conditions in which they were sustained. There

was no precedent for losses on this scale. The last decisive victory won by the British Army on the Continent of Europe had been Waterloo, where the British
contingent numbered 23,991. The largest previous
effort of the Army had been in South Africa, where in
the first eleven months, the period that covered the
whole of the 'regular' warfare, its losses in battle were
39,785—two-thirds of those suffered on the first *day*
of the Battle of the Somme in 1916. The Second
World War did not reproduce—for Britain—the holo-
causts of the First : for the whole war, 1939-1945, the
Army's losses were less than in the fighting of 1918.
Thus the First World War was a unique and revolutionary experience in British history; a nation used to
enjoying all the advantages of Imperialism and Great-
Power Status at a low cost, through the exercise of
naval supremacy, discovered with a shock the price
that had to be paid when that supremacy was no
longer effective. For, in a sentence, the final meaning
of all these daunting figures, all the huge numbers of
men engaged and lost in battle, and the very small
numbers of the miles and yards gained, was this :
British naval supremacy had ended, and Britain had
become a land power, one among many, not by any
means the strongest.

In 1914 Britain was still the supreme naval power,
with only a tiny standing Army. Her value in an
alliance, her 'great deterrent', lay in her mighty Fleet,
which had not been challenged since Trafalgar. As late
as the close of the century she had been able to disre-
gard the almost unanimous opprobrium of Europe
over the South African War, and virtually denude her-

self of troops to wage that distant campaign, behind
the shield of the Navy. It was the German Kaiser's
fleet-building, more than anything else, that drew her
into the Entente with France and into the morasses of
continental politics. The building of the German Fleet
was a gesture that could point in only one direction,
and to which the modern developments of naval con-
struction lent an unexpected probability of success.
For, just as the coming of steam had rendered all
existing navies obsolete, so the launching of H.M.S.
Dreadnought in 1906 put all major ship-building
nations on an equal footing as regards battleships. And
battleships were still the core of the Navy.

It was in May 1912 that the implications of these
two factors began to be acutely felt, and when the first
symptom of weakening was seen in Britain's most
valued weapon. In order to meet the German threat
in the North Sea the Admiralty withdrew battleships
from the Mediterranean; the effect was that Britain no
longer commanded the Imperial lifeline between Gib-
raltar and the Suez Canal. Informed opinion was
deeply disturbed; at the War Office, Henry Wilson,
Director of Military Operations, wrote in his diary :

> 'We have . . . 25 Dreadnoughts in the North
> Sea. The Germans likewise 25. Our 8 from the
> Mediterranean will make 33. . . . The net result is
> that we can *just* hold our own in the North Sea,
> and the Mediterranean is gone. This is a most par-
> lous condition of affairs.'

Parlous as it was, there was an even graver defect in
the Royal Navy at that time.

Although—indeed, perhaps because—it had enjoyed an unchallenged supremacy for over a century, the Royal Navy had produced no theoretician with a doctrine of war that would serve as a common ground for all its officers, and as an accepted point of departure for statesmen and soldiers. It was left to the American Admiral Mahan to study and analyse the campaigns of Nelson and the influence of sea-power on history. Britain produced no naval Clausewitz, nor even a Hamley, to concentrate her unique store of tactical and strategic experience into principles that would command the attention to which the Navy was entitled.

The reason for this is not far to seek : authoritative doctrines of war emerge from a consensus of professional opinion. Such a consensus is embodied in a General Staff, and there was no naval General Staff until 1912. The Navy, in fact, until then resembled the Army before the Cardwell Reforms : just as the Army had consisted of a collection of generals and regiments, the Navy consisted of a collection of admirals and ships. The corporate central brain was lacking. The seriousness of this situation became apparent during the Agadir crisis in 1911; and Lord Haldane, then Secretary for War, tells how, at a meeting of the Defence Committee presided over by the Prime Minister to discuss mobilisation arrangements, an astounding discrepancy emerged between the plans of the War Office and the Admiralty. The First Sea Lord, Sir Arthur Wilson, stated the Navy's intentions :

'They wanted to take detachments of the Expedi-

tionary Force and to land them seriatim at points on
the Baltic Coast, on the northern shores of Prussia. We
of the War Office at once said that such a plan was
from a military point of view hopeless, because the
railway system which the great General Staff of Germany had evolved was such that any division we
landed, even if the Admiralty could have got it to a
point suitable for debarkation, would be promptly
surrounded by five to ten times the number of enemy
troops. Sir John Fisher appeared to have derived the
idea from the analogy of the Seven Years' War, more
than 150 years previously, and Sir Arthur Wilson, his
successor, had apparently adopted it. The First Lord
backed him up. I said at once that the mode of em-
ploying troops and their numbers and places of operation were questions for the War Office General Staff
and that we had worked them out with the French.
The results had been periodically approved in the
Committee of Defence itself. Sir William Nicholson
(then C.I.G.S.) asked Sir Arthur whether they had at
the Admiralty a map of the German strategic railways.
Sir Arthur replied that it was not their business to have
such maps. "I beg your pardon," said Sir William,
"if you meddle with military problems you are bound
not only to have them, but to have studied them."
The discussion became sharp . . .'

Very shortly after this incident Mr. Winston
Churchill was appointed First Lord of the Admiralty,
with the task, bluntly, of dragging naval thinking and
organisation into the twentieth century. A naval staff
was created, and certain valuable new doctrines were

evolved and implemented—in particular the doctrine
of remote blockade, with the necessity of hastening the
building of new bases in the Orkneys and on the East
coast. The great base at Scapa Flow was only just
sufficiently prepared to receive the Fleet when war
broke out. Indeed, Churchill and his assistants, called
too late to their work, were caught in a trap that was
shortly to engulf the Army too. The sheer magnitude
of their material task, the urgent need to build new
ships and bases and train the men for them, drew off
energy from the intellectual effort that needed also to
be made. But in any case there was simply not enough
time to evolve balanced doctrines; it requires decades,
not months, to produce a valid theory of war.

This, then, was the true state of naval affairs in an
Empire that depended on its naval supremacy. What
of the Army? Here the picture was significantly different. The Army had had all its weaknesses—and they
were many—exposed in South Africa. Succeeding
governments and their supporters were clear that reform was needed. When the Liberals came to power in
1905 the process received a new impetus. This was the
more extraordinary since the Liberal Party was
thoroughly permeated with pacifism, and entertained
the deepest distrust of militarism in all its forms. A
significant snippet of conversation was recorded as Sir
Henry Campbell-Bannerman carried out the formation of his Government; it went as follows: 'I said,
"What about the War Office?" "Nobody," answered
Campbell-Bannerman, "will touch it with a pole."
"Then give it to me . . .".' The speaker had his wish;
he was Mr. Haldane, and by the end of his remark-

able tenure of office three major reforms in the Army had been brought to completion : a General Staff was firmly lodged in control; the Expeditionary Force had been organised; the Territorial Army had been created.

Haldane was a man of alarming intellectual prowess. He studied philosophy at Edinburgh and Goettingen Universities; he declined a professorial chair at Edinburgh and turned to law. Having mastered this new subject with sufficient thoroughness to earn about £20,000 a year, he entered politics. He joined up with Asquith and Grey, and together they formed the core of the Liberal Imperialist group whose views were regarded askance by the bulk of the Party, but whose intellectual eminence thrust them inevitably to the top.

Haldane's previous career at no point contained any link with military affairs. He stunned his first meeting of the Army Council, when he was asked what type of Army he envisaged, with the reply, 'An Hegelian Army.' 'The discussion', he remarks, 'then fell away.' He was the greatest Secretary of State for War that Britain has ever had. But underlying all his work was a fatal weakness for which he was in no way responsible. His approach to his task was from first principles. 'What is the Army for? What role must it fulfil?' were his questions. Having received his answer, and being satisfied with it, he implemented it with an unrivalled thoroughness. It was the total absence of any equally clear thinking, any similarly cogent answer on the naval side to balance against the Army view, that marred his achievement. For, in the existing context of

German belligerence, and of the closening relationship with France, the answer to these fundamental questions that Haldane accepted as his working basis was this: 'To fight beside the French Army in the event of German aggression.' It was to this end that all his work was directed; it was for this purpose that the Regular Army was reorganised into six divisions to constitute an Expeditionary Force, and the Territorials were organised as a second line to replace the regulars in all their normal duties and supplement them in the field.

The man most closely concerned in working out this concept was the ardently Francophile Irishman, Henry Wilson, Director of Military Operations from 1910 to 1914. He tells how, on one of his periodic pilgrimages to the battlefields of 1870, he reverently laid at the foot of the statue of France at Mars-la-Tour a fragment of a map showing the proposed area of concentration of the British Army in France in the event of war—an odd procedure on many counts, not least that of security. But odder still is the fact that this was the only war plan that Britain possessed when she entered the War on August 4th, 1914.

When the War broke out, a further complication was added: the new Secretary of State for War, Lord Kitchener. Kitchener discerned at once, through those processes of personal intuition on which he had depended all his life, what no Staff Officer[1] nor politician fully perceived, that the War would be a long one, at least three years, and that Britain must have a very large Army to wage it. He set about raising this Army immediately. 'Even if Lord Kitchener had done nothing more than this,' remarks Lord Esher, one of his severest critics, 'his taking office would have been an inestimable service to the country. . . .'

Kitchener's conception of the New Armies has been generally treated as a masterpiece of organisation; in fact, it was the opposite. One of his best friends, Sir Ian Hamilton, has written, 'he hated organisations; he smashed organisations. . . .' This would seem to be the truth. For Lord Kitchener, contrary to popular belief, was not a military 'expert'; he was not a qualified Staff Officer. He was a leader, with brilliant intuition and mastery of expedient, and immense force of character. The whole of his career in the Army was spent overseas, in Egypt, South Africa and India. Everything that he did was a personal endeavour; he scarcely knew how to delegate, nor did he believe in the machinery of office. As General Rawlinson, who served on his tiny staff in the Sudan campaign in 1898, said, 'The one serious criticism that I have is that this is too much a one-man show.' Drawing on his huge reserves of mental and physical energy, Kitchener made everything he touched a one-man show. It worked in the Sudan; it worked (more or less) in South Africa; it set things moving in the congealed conditions of India during the first decade of the century. But applied to the overwhelming problems of modern war in Europe in 1914 it would not do.

Kitchener was entirely unfamiliar with European armies and military organisation. Intuition told him what needed to be done. All his practical experience tended to draw him into wrong methods of doing it. The raising of the New Armies—his greatest achievement—is a case in point. Nothing could have been more personal than the manner in which he set about this. 'Your country needs you!' roared the posters, beside a picture of Kitchener. Battalions, whole brigades, sprang into being at Lord Kitchener's word, or at the stroke of his pen. The story of the 23rd (Sportsman's) Battalion of the Royal Fusiliers, if not typical, is indicative: 'That popular sportswoman, Mrs. E. Cunliffe-Owen . . . on chaffing some of her friends towards the end of August on not being in khaki, was challenged to raise a battalion of middle- and upper-class men up to the age of forty-five. She promptly . . . telegraphed to Lord Kitchener, "Will you accept complete battalion of upper- and middle-class men, physically fit, able to shoot and ride, up to the age of forty-five?" The answer came promptly back, "Lord Kitchener gratefully accepts complete battalion." Mrs. Cunliffe-Owen got to work at once. The India Room at the Hotel Cecil was engaged as a recruiting depot. . . . Mrs. Cunliffe-Owen, seated behind a screen, signed the papers herself. A triumph.' By such means as these the First Hundred Thousand was raised, and the hundreds of thousands of volunteers who came after them. As Lord Esher commented: 'Since it was conceded that the War would be fought under a system of voluntary enlistment and unequal sacrifice . . . it is more than doubtful whether armies could have been raised by any method other than the one he chose.' But this was a concession, adds Lord Esher, for which England was destined to pay a heavy price. That price is still being paid today.

The immediate cost of the personal method was a

double one. First, it involved the complete setting aside
of the Territorial system which Lord Haldane had envisaged as the natural manner of expanding the Army,
through the County Associations. Instead of using this
excellent machinery, and turning to best account the
existing Territorial divisions, Kitchener preferred to
add another category of entirely raw troops to the
Army, thereby hampering the Territorials severely in
reaching their full utility. The reason for his rejection
of the Territorial system is interesting. Having taken
part in the Franco-Prussian War, he had grimly vivid
memories of the French Territorial troops in 1870-
1871. He entirely ignored the fact that the British
Territorials of 1914, enthusiastic, mainly young, citizen soldiers, were utterly different from the old French
reservists who shared their title. Such is the power of a
word, and such is the cost of the personal method.

But even more serious was his refusal to throw the
huge weight of his prestige behind compulsory service.
The result of adhering to the voluntary method was
that the Kitchener Armies skimmed off the best blood
in the country, the most ardent, the mentally, spiritu-
ally and physically most active, leaving very little,
when they were expended, to leaven the masses that
must follow. The sequel of the story of the 23rd Royal
Fusiliers is revealing. In one hut at their first camp,
says their historian, 'the first bed was occupied by the
brother of a peer. The second by the man who drove
his car. . . . Other beds were occupied by a mechanical
engineer, and old Blundell's School boy, planters, a
mine overseer from Scotland, a man in possession of a
flying pilot's certificate . . . an old sea-dog who had

rounded the Cape Horn on no fewer than nine occasions, a man who had hunted seals . . .' No doubt this
was splendidly democratic; but one senses a waste of
talent, and one learns without surprise that 'with this
as with other high-class battalions the number of men
taking commissions proved a serious drain on its
strength . . .' The New Armies themselves, the Army
as a whole, and ultimately the nation, were all gravely
injured by this haphazard, improvised method of recruiting. But there was worse to follow when the
question arose of how the New Armies were to be
used.

Whatever may have been the merits or demerits of
the strategy of conveying the British Expeditionary
Force to France immediately on the outbreak of war,
there can be no question about the efficiency with
which it was carried out. Mobilisation proceeded
smoothly; concentration was ahead of schedule; security was astonishingly complete. It is no criticism of the
B.E.F., nor of its organisation and training, that it was
instantly involved in a débâcle which came very near
to being fatal. The criticism must be against the absence of positive thinking that allowed the military
effort of the Empire to follow at the heels of French
strategic doctrine. The result was the retreat from
Mons, with its sequel, the Marne, and the 'Race to the
Sea'. This last operation represented the sole possibility
that ever existed of a great turning movement on the
Western Front. It ended at Ypres, in October 1914,
where the French and British forces, vainly supposing
that they were about to turn the northern flank, met
huge masses of enemy troops who were intending to

perform a similar feat. By heroic exertions, which brought about the almost total destruction of the original British Expeditionary Force, the Allies were able to hold the Germans at bay outside Ypres, and dig in along a line that thereafter stretched unbroken from the Channel to Switzerland.

Two permanent results stemmed from this fighting in 1914. The first was the increasing clamour that then arose, and continued until the very end of the War, for reinforcements to the Western Front. The French Army is known to have lost 374,000 men in the three months of September, October and November. Its losses in August have never been officially stated, though some have put them as high as 300,000 men in the first ten days of the War; they must have been immense, since they included those of the disastrous Battles of the Frontiers, which exposed the fatal fallacies underlying the French doctrine of offensive at all costs. These human losses, coupled with the loss of the occupied Northern provinces, not unnaturally produced a certain frame of mind in Frenchmen. The desire to expel the invader, and to avenge the outrages that he had committed, assumed a tremendous force.

In the context of early 1915, with this determination (shared by many Englishmen) ascendant in France, and with almost every reputable military leader convinced that the drawn battles of 1914 were artificial and impermanent results, the endless argument about 'The Line' made its appearance. The French insisted that the British must take over more front: they must release French divisions for the offensive if they could not attack themselves; preferably they would take over more front *and* attack themselves, alongside the French. In view of France's losses it was hard to resist these demands. In any case, they were supported by British G.H.Q., which had its own defeats and injuries to avenge. But these emotional inclinations, however comprehensible, had little relevance to the stark tactical reality of deadlock which was the other result of 1914. With the equipment of the Allied armies of 1915, and, indeed, much later, there was no solution to the problem of assaulting successive trench positions, protected by barbed wire and defended by machine-guns and massed artillery.

This was the moment when the hiatus in British pre-war strategic thinking was exposed : for it was now, at the beginning of 1915, the great German gamble having failed, that Britain should have been able to exert the large influence due to her naval supremacy. For only naval power, with its opportunity for amphibious attacks, could tilt the balance that had been arrived at in the field. It was not, of course, that no one perceived this : but it was too late to have to begin trying to re-orientate the whole strategy of the Allies. 1911 would have been the latest moment to commence the laborious process of talking the French out of their delusion; but as we have seen, there was a total lack of understanding between the War Office and the Admiralty in 1911. Consequently the belated attempt to revive a truly maritime strategy was doomed to failure.[2]

Indeed, there was no real agreement among the British leaders themselves about such a strategy. Sir John French, the Commander-in-Chief of the B.E.F.,

and the bulk of the General Staff Officers, not unnaturally, since they were now serving in France, clung
to the view that this was the only front that mattered.
Lord Kitchener, on the other hand, inspired again by
his almost infallible intuition, wrote to French on
January 2nd:

> 'I suppose we must now recognise that the French
> Army cannot make a sufficient break through the
> German lines to bring about the retreat of the Ger-
> man forces from Northern Belgium. If that is so,
> then the German lines in France may be looked on
> as a fortress that cannot be carried by assault and
> also that cannot be completely invested, with the
> result that the lines may be held by an investing
> force, whilst operations proceed elsewhere.'

At the same time, Sir John Fisher, now First Sea
Lord again, was reviving his ideas for attacks on Germany's northern coasts. Colonel Hankey, Secretary to
the Committee of Imperial Defence, was suggesting a
blow against Germany's new ally, Turkey. Mr. Lloyd
George, Chancellor of the Exchequer, was for withdrawing the bulk of the B.E.F. from France and des-
patching it to a new theatre, unspecified; later he
became especially enamoured of the possibilities of
Salonika. Into this confusion of counsel Mr. Winston
Churchill, First Lord of the Admiralty, threw, with all
the persuasive force at his command, the idea of an
attack on the Dardanelles.

There was nothing new about this idea; it did not
emanate from a Churchillian brainstorm. Ever since
the probability of an alliance between Turkey and

Germany had been envisaged the question of forcing the Dardanelles straits and attacking Constantinople had been considered. In 1904, 1906, 1908, and again in 1911, the General Staff had surveyed the problem, and had finally reached the conclusion that '*without surprise* any attempt to land an army on the Gallipoli peninsula would be too hazardous'. Such was the chaos of British war planning, under its various pulls and stresses, that it would appear that no attention was paid to these earlier examinations of the problem. Certainly the conditions laid down in them for success were totally ignored. Yet the potential value of this campaign was beyond question greater than that of any other operation undertaken by the Allies until the final campaign of 1918. Sir William Robertson, who as Chief of Staff to Sir John French at that time, and later as C.I.G.S., bitterly opposed the Dardanelles campaign, has recognised its promise as clearly as anyone :

> 'The advantages to be derived from forcing the Straits were perfectly obvious. Such a success would, as the advocates of the project have said, serve to secure Egypt, to induce Italy and the Balkan States to come in on our side, and, if followed by the forcing of the Bosphorus, would enable Russia to draw munitions from America and Western Europe, and to export her accumulated supplies of wheat.'

One can add that success would also have offered the only possibility of uniting the Eastern and Western Fronts, with the further chance of staving off the Russian Revolution. Brigadier J. E. Edmonds, the

British Official Historian, a consistent supporter of the 'Western Front' policy, as opposed to all 'sideshows' has written :

'In view of the situation on the Western Front and the subsequent failures of the French and British offensives in 1915, the wisdom of the decision to make trial elsewhere—provided that surprise was ensured—can hardly be questioned.'

And the Official Historian of the Gallipoli campaign itself adds :

'There can be still less doubt that in the spring of 1915 the operation was not beyond the capacity of the Entente, and that a combined naval and military attack, carefully planned in every detail before troops embarked, and carried out with the essential advantages of surprise, would have succeeded.'

These were the very desiderata that did not exist. The story of the campaign is the story of a series of opportunities missed by inches. The historian of Gallipoli sums it up in this conclusion : 'Many reasons combined to frustrate an enterprise the success of which in 1915 would have altered the course of the war. But every reason will be found to spring from one fundamental cause—an utter lack of preparation before the campaign began.' At the root of this lack of preparation lay the long-standing absence of accord between the General Staff and the Admiralty. It was because of this that the idea originated with the Admiralty, and was conceived at first as a purely naval venture. Lord Kitchener stated categorically that he had no troops to offer. When, inevitably, it was recognised that the Army must come in, the troops were scraped together. There were just too few of them; reinforcements were belatedly sent, but always just too few. Finally, almost half a million Allied soldiers were sent to Gallipoli, but after the initial loss of surprise they were always too few and too late to swing the balance. By sickness and battle the British Army lost over 200,000 men in this unhappy, but potentially decisive, campaign. Brigadier J. E. Edmonds makes the lesson clear : '. . . Once the decision was reached . . . all attacks in the West on a large scale—at any rate by the B.E.F.—should have been prohibited; for in 1915 there were neither the munitions nor the men to sustain two serious efforts with any hope of bringing either of them to a successful conclusion.'

Even with this proviso, one must question whether the Gallipoli venture could have succeeded in 1915. As has been shown, the French were in no mood for a suspension of offensives on the Western Front. Could they ever have been convinced, at this late stage? And what of the enemy? Just three days before the first landing at Gallipoli, the Germans launched the first gas attack. This operation, the Second Battle of Ypres, was one of the great crises of the War. The strain imposed on the British Army was very great, and its urgent demands for reinforcements and munitions could scarcely have been refused. In short, one is forced to the conclusion that Gallipoli could only have succeeded in terms of a clearly stated intention, long before the War, to use the bulk of Britain's reserves amphibiously, and in terms of an agreement by France to shape her strategy accordingly.

The failure of the Gallipoli campaign meant the failure of sea-power itself. This was Britain's last great adventure as a supreme maritime state—her last attempt to use sea-power as a decisive weapon. For the remainder of the 1914-1918 War Britain's main effort was lodged in the Army fighting on the Continent of Europe, and depending on the Navy only for main-tenance and supply. By November 1918, nearly five and a half million British troops had been sent to France and Flanders. Kitchener's brave New Armies were the first of these hosts to enter the new type of warfare that now began. Their great test was the Battle of the Somme in 1916. On the first day of the fighting, July 1st, the British Army sustained 57,000 casualties. In the four and a half months that the battle continued it lost 415,000 men. This was by far the most terrible ordeal in its history. The Official Historian says: '. . . the real war of attrition starts with the assumption by the British Armies on the Somme of the leading role in the fighting on the Western Front.' Sir Winston Churchill has added: 'The battlefields of the Somme were the graveyards of Kitchener's Army.'

The tragedy of the Somme goes even beyond this loss of life. Its immediate effects were, first, to thrust Britain into an undesirable military leadership, which she had to sustain thereafter; and, secondly, to sow the seeds of deep distrust between soldiers and politi-cians that bedevilled her effort throughout the rest of the War. In the post-war years most of the disillusion and pacifism which grew up arose out of memories of the slaughter on the Somme. In the Second World War many of the inhibitions of British strategy, and differences between British and American Staffs, were derived from these same memories, and the fact that America had had no Sommes. Today a poverty of inspiration is discernible in the age-group that guides the country, through the extinction of a whole generation of talent on the Somme. Because of the turn that the War took when Gallipoli failed, and attrition took the place of manœuvre, peace itself brought little comfort. Again it was Sir Winston Churchill who defined the quality of the Armistice of 1918 :

'No splendid harmony was to crown the wonderful achievements. No prize was to reward the sacrifices of the combatants. Victory was to be bought so dear as to be almost indistinguishable from defeat. It was not to give even security to the victors. . . . The most complete victory ever gained in arms has failed to solve the European problem or remove the dangers which produced the war.'

In other words, the manner in which the Great War was fought after 1916 has decided the nature of the century we live in.

NOTES

1. Not quite true : see pp 58, 219, 221.

2. As will be seen, during the two years which elapsed between the writing of this essay and the next, my opinions on this subject changed considerably.

THE GENESIS
OF THE WESTERN FRONT

Because of its particular horrors, the Western Front of
1914-1918 has come to occupy a special place in the
minds of people who read history. There is a general
awareness of the vast scale of the Allied effort on that
front throughout the First World War, of the immen-
sity of the losses sustained there under frequently
hideous conditions, and of the bitter controversy that
has raged ever since about the need for either the effort
or the loss—a controversy not stilled by the popular
demand for the 'Second Front', and its decisive success in the same arena during the Second World War.
Yet in 1944 the problem was complicated by the fact
that an opposed landing had to be made before a
Western Front could even come into existence, while
in 1914 the Allied riposte at the Marne established
that front without interruption as the permanent
major theatre of war. This is a contradiction, that
seems likely to engage historians for many more years
to come. At the root of all the controversy there may
well lie, as with so many of the complex and difficult
passages in human affairs, a terrible simplicity.

Free will is not often granted to governments at
critical times, and this fact was well illustrated at the
outbreak of war in 1914. It may be as well to recall
some of the chronology surrounding the event. The

Central Powers, Germany and Austria, declared war against Serbia on July 28th, against Russia on August 1st, against France on August 3rd and Belgium on August 4th. Formal war was not declared upon Great Britain until November 23rd, when actual hostilities had been in progress for nearly four months. The Russians were almost as dilatory with their declaration against the Central Powers—November 3rd. But France had made her gesture on August 3rd, and Belgium on August 4th, in immediate response to the dangers that menaced them. The German invasion of Belgium was simultaneous with the declaration of war, and it was this invasion that decided Great Britain's action. General mobilisation of the Army was ordered, and the final British ultimatum sent to the German Government on August 4th. The ultimatum expired at midnight, and fifteen minutes later the Foreign Office issued the statement that Britain and Germany were at war. The declaration was officially back-dated by one day, but in fact this meant that Britain went to war with Germany on August 5th, two days after France, while her mobilisation only began three days after that of her ally.

The cause of these discrepancies and delays was the habitual disadvantage that confronts relatively unwarlike democracies when faced with resolute action by determined military powers. A substantial part of the German Army was maintained permanently on a war footing, but even more important was the fact that the military machine was so built into the organisation of the state that its functions could be performed without arousing particular attention. This was not the case in France, and still less so in England. In order not to cause provocation or alarm, as late as July 30th, the French Government was ordering that no special railway movements should be made by the Army, no reservists should be called up, and no requisitions should be made. The French covering forces were instructed that they must not pass beyond a line drawn ten kilometres from the frontier.[1] The British Fleet, fortunately, was able to move straight from its annual manœuvres to its war stations in comparative secrecy. But this did not apply to the Army, which could scarcely shift a unit without causing disturbance and drawing attention. Thus both governments held back from the act of mobilisation which, once committed, could only progressively weaken their power to control events. By August 1st, however, France could delay no longer. Already, through the relative development of their preparations, the Germans had seized a valuable initiative.[2] The continued hesitation of the British Liberal Government, though perfectly intelligible, and possibly praiseworthy in terms of moral rectitude, nevertheless created extra damage by sowing the seeds of understandable doubt in France. The need to allay French anxiety certainly played a considerable part in shaping the deliberations and decisions that followed.

The nature of those deliberations and decisions was characteristic of the age. At 4 p.m. on August 5th the Prime Minister, Mr. Asquith, summoned a Council of War at No. 10 Downing Street. Not only its proceedings but its constitution were significant. All accounts of it by those who took part convey a strong air of: 'Well, gentlemen, we seem to have landed ourselves in this War. Has anyone any views on what ought to be done about it?' And in the civilised traditions of British Government and Liberalism, the gentlemen so addressed were a far-flung cross-section of available expert opinion; astonishingly far-flung, when one considers the agenda before them.

The Prime Minister was in the chair, a position to which he was eminently suited. The Foreign Secretary, Sir Edward Grey, was present—reasonably enough. There was also the Lord Chancellor, Lord Haldane, briefly holding the reins at the War Office, where Mr. Asquith himself had been in charge for the past few months.[3] The following day Lord Kitchener was appointed Secretary of State; in the meantime Lord Haldane's counsel was of special value, in view of his great work in that office. Lord Kitchener himself was also present—the country's most eminent serving soldier, snatching a short leave from his Eastern preoccupations. There was Mr. Winston Churchill, the First Lord of the Admiralty. And the two political representatives of the Service Ministries were supported by their chief professional subordinates, the First Sea Lord, Prince Louis of Battenberg, and the Chief of Imperial General Staff, Sir Charles Douglas. Also representing the Army was Field-Marshal Sir John French, who had just been appointed Commander-in-Chief of the British Expeditionary Force, and whose presence was therefore not unreasonable. But with him was mustered an astonishing array of lesser beings.

It seems odd now that, with the C.I.G.S. present, the Commander-in-Chief should have been requested to bring with him his own Chief of Staff and Sub-Chief of Staff, Generals Sir Archibald Murray and Henry Wilson, and his two Army Corps commanders, Sir Douglas Haig and Sir James Grierson. In addition to all these, the Army was also represented by the Quartermaster-General to the Forces, Sir John Cowans, the Master-General of Ordnance, Sir Stanley von Donop, and the Inspector-General of the Overseas Forces, Sir Ian Hamilton. Finally, there was the formidable figure of Lord Roberts of Kandahar, eighty-two years old, renowned and eager.

The thought of such a gathering offends against every modern conception of war direction; it is almost impossible to imagine what they could usefully have discussed at this stage, in view of the very different levels of their information and responsibility. What they did discuss was, first, where should the B.E.F. be sent? and, secondly, what should it consist of? Since these were both elementary questions which had been under consideration and had received their answers in the very act of creating the Expeditionary Force years before, the discussion that followed could scarcely fail to be confusing, and it is not to be wondered at that no two accounts of it by participants agree. It is, however, clear that at this meeting there was practically no attempt at any fundamental last-minute revision of strategy; there was no full-scale discussion of the wisdom or probable consequences of committing Britain's whole military effort to the Continent at the outset of the struggle. Not one person in this strangely assorted, but unquestionably authoritative, assembly of naval, military and political talent doubted that the proper

Ostende
°Antwerp
Bruges
Ghent
Dunkerque
Calais
6th French Army (Degoutte)
Belgian Army
(Sixt. v. Armin)
BRUSSELS
2
French
Portuguese
St Omer
(Plumer)
Boulogne
Portuguese
Lille
(v. Quast)
BELG
5
(Birdwood)
Tournai
Mons
Etaples
Bethune
(Otto v. Below)
Charleroi
Montreuil
French Cavalry moving north
1
Arras
Douai
Maubeuge
BRITISH ARMY
(HAIG)
(Horne)
(v. der Marwitz)
v. BOEHN
Doullens
3
Vulnoye
Abbeville
(Byng)
Albert
(v. Hutier)
CROWN
4 American
Hirson
(Rawlinson)
(v. Carlowitz)
Amiens
7 (v. Eberhardt)
M
Montdidier
(v. Mudra)
(v.
(Debeney)
Laon
Compiègne
Rethel
Soissons
G. A. FAYOLLE
10
(Mangin)
Italians
Reims
Château-Thierry
Châlons
5
4
(Berthelot)
(Gouraud
PARIS
G. A. MAISTRE

F   R   A   N   C   E

Scale of Miles
0   10   20   40   60   80

SITUATION ON SEPT 25TH 1918
American Divisions
Cavalry   „
Landwehr   „
Other   „
Railways

German Divs in Reserve
Fresh
Tired

Front Line 17th July ....

HOLLAND

Liége

BELGIUM

Marche

GERMANY

Austrian

V. GALLWITZ

Montmédy   Luxembourg

5
(v. François)

Austrian

C.Del
(Fuche)   Thionville

19
(v. Bothmer)

DUKE ALBRECHT OF WURTTEMBURG

Metz

Austrian

2

French

St Mihiel   French

'A' Det   Strassbourg

Nancy

AMERICAN ARMY
(PERSHING)

8
(Gérard)

American
Epinal

G. A. DE CASTELNAU

7
Boissoudy

American

'B' Det.
(v. Gundell)

American

SWITZERLAND

destination of the B.E.F. was North-western Europe. What did exercise them was the question whether, in view of the fact that our mobilisation was already three days behind the French, and that the Germans were striking at Belgium, some reconsideration of detail might be necessary; whether, in fact, Antwerp might not be a better point for the B.E.F. to make for than Maubeuge.

There was, of course, no possible alternative to France or Flanders. Not only had the whole organisation and planning of the Expeditionary Force been based from the beginning on the idea of fighting beside the French Army, but the Entente Cordiale itself largely rested on this concept. The three-day delay that preceded the Council of War had already had serious results in France, which the French Ambassador had not hesitated to emphasise. The War Office planners, who were responsible for the mobilisation and assembly of the B.E.F., were equally perturbed at the disruption of careful schedules that had been caused. Ever since the institution of Staff talks between the two countries in 1906, although it had been carefully stated that these talks were not to be binding upon the governments, there had been an inevitable progress towards this moment, the moment of truth—and impotence—for the Government of Great Britain.

For a short time in 1906, there had existed the possibility of setting a different strategy in train. France, at that time, felt very unsure of herself. Her only ally, Russia, had just suffered a heavy defeat at the hands of Japan. Her own army was still affected by the Dreyfus schism, and was a much less powerful instrument than it became by 1914. Her desire for British support was deep, and expressed with none of the arrogance that later became habitual in joint discussions of military affairs. Faced with German threats over the Moroccan crisis, the French were naturally eager to know how Britain proposed to act; and this was a difficult question to answer, because the crisis coincided with the General Election that brought the Liberal Party to power. The Liberal Foreign Secretary-designate, Sir Edward Grey, intimated that he had no intention of departing from the Anglo-French agreement signed by his predecessor, Lord Landsdowne. But the terms of this agreement were very general, and said nothing about military action. It was in order to arrive at some kind of clarification of this aspect that Colonel Repington, Military Correspondent of *The Times,* in consultation with Lord Esher and Sir George Clarke, Secretary of the Defence Committee, took it upon himself, as a responsible but unofficial person, to sound out the French Government on the form of military collaboration between the two Powers that they envisaged. The answers would then be put before the appropriate British authorities as a working basis.

On January 5th, 1906, Colonel Repington addressed eleven questions to the French Government; on January 12th Major Huguet, the French Military Attaché in London, brought him the answers that had been provided by the French Prime Minister and the Minister of War. Repington's first question was:

‘Have the *Conseil Supérieur de la Guerre* considered British co-operation in case of war with

Germany? In what manner do they consider this co-operation can best be carried out : (a) by sea, (b) by land?'

The French answered this in reverse order :

'The question of co-operation with the British Army on land has been studied—it is considered that, to be most useful, its action should : (a) be joined to that of the French Army, that is to say, be placed under the same direction, *whether the two armies act in the same theatre of operations, or in different theatres,*[4] (b) make itself felt at the opening of hostilities, because of the considerable moral effect that would result from that. . . . At sea, England's special position, the large superiority of her fleet, her ability to take all necessary preparatory measures in advance, *enable her to form a plan better than France,*[5] which does not enjoy the same freedom of action . . .'

In this part of their reply to Repington's first question, and in other replies, the French made it clear that they looked for a lead from the world's greatest naval power. Question 6 was :

'Do the French look to us to propose a plan of joint action by sea? Have they any plan ready to suggest to us?'

The answer was simply :

'See reply to first question.'

In their reply to Question 8, which was about the

disposal of naval and colonial captures, the French said :

'However, *a priori,* it seems likely that, since England is likely to play the most brilliant part in this matter, France will give way entirely to what England decides.'

To the question :

'Should we establish it as a principle . . . that the English shall command at sea and the French on land?'

the reply was :

'Yes; unity of direction being absolutely essential whether on land or at sea.'

Even as regards land operations, within the concept of unified direction, the French preserved considerable fluidity in 1906. Repington's fourth question anticipated the events that actually took place eight years later :

'Assuming that Germany violates Belgian territory what plan of operations do the French propose for co-operation between the French, English and Belgian forces?'

The French did not set much store by the possibility of Belgium vigorously defending her territory; they went on :

'In the event of her deciding to defend her soil, immediate common action, under unified direction, would be proposed—action which cannot be defined beforehand, because it will depend on circumstances.'

The circumstances which no one could have predicted, and which is still a matter for wonder, was that the British Government would refrain from making any counter-proposals; would take no steps to give full strategic effect to the Supreme Command at sea that was conceded so frankly by the French; and would permit a small group of Staff Officers to interpret the joint action on land, which was then so loosely defined by the French, in its narrowest sense.

There were many reasons for all this. The period of the great reform of the British Army, during which both the Expeditionary Force and the General Staff were given their shape, was just about to begin, and the sheer magnitude of the task diverted much energy and talent from the co-ordination of strategic studies. The Navy was even later in tackling its reorganisation, and meanwhile operated under a series of autocracies, of which the most notable was that of Sir John Fisher, the First Sea Lord in 1906. On the day after the French Government's reply to Repington's questionnaire was received, Sir George Clarke interviewed Fisher on the subject of naval plans and, says Repington, 'telephoned to me that his talk had been very unsatisfactory, and that Fisher was not prepared to meet the French half-way . . . Admiral Fisher, said Sir. G. Clarke, would not let the French into any plans of ours. . .' Old habits die hard. France had been the British Navy's traditional enemy for centuries, and Fisher's reaction was instinctive. On the other side of the Channel the same frame of mind operated. When Major Huguet visited the Operations Bureau of the French General Staff to ask them about co-operation with the British, 'he found them deeply engaged upon the elaboration of an academic plan for the invasion of England, and when he told them of the friendly British invasion which some of us contemplated, their jaws dropped, their pens fell from their hands, and they were positively transfixed with surprise'.

It is now clear that the fatal defect of the period was the absence until a late date of a true General Staff in either of the two Services, let alone a joint Staff to co-ordinate their plans. Indeed, the latter had to wait until the Second World War to be fashioned into an effective instrument. During the whole period between 1906 and 1914 there was no lack of strategic studies in Britain, but they were diffuse, and never brought to-gether until their results were presented as a *fait accompli* at the Council of War on the day after war was declared. The Committee of Imperial Defence had been very active. From 1907 to 1913 it undertook detailed inquiries into a wide range of problems. Indeed, Lord Oxford (Mr. Asquith) has said:

'It would not be an unjust claim to say that the Government had by [1909] investigated the whole ground covered by a possible war with Germany—the naval position; the possibilities of a blockade; the invasion problem; the continental problem; the Egyptian problem.'

It is a sad comment that, after all that hard work, the strategy of the War became a matter for bitter debate within a few months of its opening, and has remained so ever since. But by August 5th, 1914, the only question left for argument was whether the Expeditionary Force should go to Antwerp or Maubeuge, and even this was an unreal question.

Nevertheless, it is a question worth examining, in the terms in which it presented itself to those who took part in the Council of War, because the alternative, minuscule as it was, represented the last opportunity of separating the main effort of the British Army from direct subordination to the French. Sir John French, who had been C.I.G.S. until March 1914, and was therefore familiar with the Operations Branch plan (worked out mainly by Henry Wilson) to place the British Army on the left wing of the French, concentrating for that purpose at Maubeuge, wrote afterwards in his book *1914* that he was 'most anxious to adhere to our original plans'. But both Wilson and Haig, in their diaries written at the time, show that it was French who raised the possibility of going to Antwerp—'dragged in the ridiculous proposal', as Wilson put it. And Haig wrote :

'Personally, I trembled at the reckless way Sir J. French spoke about "the advantages" of the B.E.F. operating from Antwerp against the powerful and still intact German Army.'

Finally, the Antwerp proposal was overruled, despite some support from Lord Roberts, partly on the grounds that it constituted a dangerous dispersal of effort, risking defeat in detail, but mainly because the Navy could not guarantee communications across that

wider section of the North Sea. Since the approaches
to Antwerp lay inside neutral territory, the Navy's
attitude is comprehensible. The uneasiness that shortly
afterwards grew up about French's strategic capacity
probably had its origins in this proposal.

With Antwerp ruled out, there still remained a
small area of disagreement among the soldiers at the
Council of War. Lord Kitchener, for one, queried
whether Maubeuge was not too far advanced and
exposed as a concentration area for an Army whose
bases would necessarily be sea-ports. He preferred
Amiens, and Sir Ian Hamilton supported him in this.
The Corps Commanders were consulted. Grierson,
who had been among the first to initiate close Anglo-
French military co-operation, 'spoke up for decisive
numbers at the decisive point'—according to Wilson,
so this presumably meant Maubeuge. Haig then, alone
in this gathering, took the opportunity of putting forward a number of fundamental questions which, says
Wilson, 'led to our discussing strategy like idiots'.

It was Haig's misfortune that he was never a good
or impressive speaker; his questions, and the supple-
mentary points that he put forward, were anything
but idiotic. He had little faith in the offensive doctrines
that had recently become current in the French Army;
it seemed unlikely to him that their headlong attack
would succeed, and he feared the effects of the small
British Expeditionary Force being drawn into the vortex of a French defeat. On the other hand, as one of
his Staff Officers records, he was aware of an even
more immediate danger, 'that, with an Army and
nation of moral so sensitive as the French, the Alliance

itself might be endangered by alterations involving delay, and that therefore the Expeditionary Force must move in its greatest possible strength at the earliest possible moment, *and conform to the plans of the French Command*[6] in the initial stages of the war'. These views, strongly backed by Wilson, with French and Murray in agreement, won the day, and tied the last knot that bound British action to French plans.

At this War Council it was also decided that the Expeditionary Force should, as always envisaged, consist of six infantry divisions and one of cavalry—the whole striking force of Great Britain. But Lord Kitchener's misgivings steadily increased as he assumed the responsibilities of office, and the next day he modified this decision. Only two Army Corps went to France in the first wave, so that a small fraction of Britain's Regular Army was preserved from the harassment of the Retreat from Mons—only, unfortunately, to be expended on the Aisne and at Ypres. If there was one question that this oddly constituted Council of War might profitably have discussed, it was the economic use of the exiguous, but high-quality, Army that Britain possessed. Haig, indeed, urged that 'we must organise our resources *for a war of several years*',[7] Kitchener rapidly reached the same conclusion, but when it became a matter of implementing it lacked the benefit of trained Staff Officers of Haig's calibre. From this stemmed much of the sheer waste that ultimately brought valid manœuvres into such disrepute.

And so it came about that the whole of Britain's available military force became committed, from the outset, to action beside the French. The question remains, whether there was ever any real possibility afterwards of extracting the *main* strength of the Empire from the French front. Imperial commitments made it plain, also from the outset, that there would have to be other fronts, and it may be useful, at this stage, to note what proportion of the Empire's manpower they ultimately absorbed. The official statistical record lists ten major theatres of operations, besides France and Flanders, during the First World War. Unquestionably, the Western Front predominated: it swallowed up 5,399,563 men, compared with 3,576,391 for all the rest together. Yet three and half million is no small number, and further inspection reveals more of interest. Five of those ten fronts accounted for just under 250,000 men between them, so that the remaining subsidiary campaigns used over three and a quarter million. This means, in effect, that although 'subsidiary', 'secondary', or whatever adjective one may care to use, they were, in fact, pretty big affairs. Egypt and Palestine, for example, from first to last, gave employment to 1,192,511 men; Mesopotamia to 889,702; the Dardanelles to 468,987; Salonika to 404,207; and, surprisingly, East Africa to 372,950.[8] And these were only the British Empire's contribution; there was a considerable French contingent at the Dardanelles, while at Salonika the French played the larger part. But for an Empire which, at the outbreak of war, had only been able to muster an Expeditionary Force of 100,000 men, these 'sideshows' alone represented an astonishing military expansion and effort.

The key question, then, is whether, in view of this large diversion of strength to other theatres, some

further diversion might not have resulted in progress
that apart from its own positive impact on the War,
would have saved us from much of the slaughter and
misery on the Western Front. This question has been
argued endlessly from the point of view of the merits
and demerits of particular campaigns. Each one of
them had its *raison d'être* and its prospects; each contributed something to the final victory. But at this distance it seems more and more clear that underlying
them all was the unfolding of a tern reality which had
escaped discussion at the Council of War on August
5th, 1914, and in the planning that had preceded it.
For, once committed, the demands of the Expeditionary Force in France grew inevitably and inexorably.

As soon as battle was joined, the tragic errors and
weaknesses of French stategy were revealed. Against
the mass and subtlety of the famous Schlieffen Plan,
the French offensive doctrine crumbled into ruin. By
prodigious personal efforts and inflexible will-power,
Joffre was able to frustrate the object of the Schlieffen
Plan at the Battle of the Marne. But the initiative that
Germany had grasped at the very beginning brought
its reward as a by-product. Once the Western Front
was stabilised from the sea to Switzerland, enclosing
in German hands almost the whole of Belgium and
some of the most valuable provinces of France, there
was never any question whatever, as long as the
French remained the chief partners in land operations,
of this front becoming anything but the dominant
theatre. Technical military jargon can sound irritating
at times; but it contains concepts as real as those of any

other science. The reality of 1914 was that, although Germany had failed to achieve the swift decision that she had sought, she was able, by her territorial gains, to retain the initiative, and dictate the course of the War. It is perhaps less difficult to see this, if one supposes the situation in reverse.

Let us suppose that the Allied offensive in 1914 had been partially successful; that the Allies had carried their front into German territory; that they occupied some valuable part of Germany such as the Saar; but that thereafter they found themselves unable to make further progress. What then would have been their correct strategy? It would surely have been axiomatic that the main force of Germany would be riveted to the front on her national territory, and the search for a decisive 'turning' front elsewhere would have been the obvious next step. Blocked, but still holding the initiative in the West, the Allies could rightly, *if they had the strength,* have tried to 'knock away the props', as the strategy of sideshows was called. For 'knocking away the props' requires two things: the initiative, and strength. But Germany held the initiative and, indeed, enough strength to knock away certain Allied 'props', namely Serbia and Roumania, and ultimately, with the not inconsiderable aid of internal revolution, Russia. But she had not enough strength to knock out Russia until the Revolution assisted her; nor did she ever have the strength to knock out Italy. The Allies, by 1916, when Russia was still able to make a last impressive stroke, and the Kitchener Armies were coming into the field in force, probably had the strength to destroy at least one of Germany's allies;

but they did not have the initiative, and were forced
to spend their strength in other ways. The valuable
attribute of initiative, lost in 1914, had, indeed, been
even further removed by the events of 1915.

All through that year, France danced to the German
tune; her armies were launched repeatedly, as it was
inevitable that they would be, against the invaders of
her territory. It is well-nigh impossible to imagine anything that could have prevented this from happening—
except a long-standing agreement with Great Britain
to do something based on British sea-power, and
backed by a far greater British land contribution than
was then available. Even so, the greater probability is
that France would have pleaded her special needs, and
thrown her strength against the German lines in the
West. The British Expeditionary Force, fighting beside
the French, was drawn into their actions and their
dangers. It grew steadily as the pressure of French demands upon it grew; it absorbed more and more of
the man-power and equipment which, with dire
struggles, the country was making available. The para-
dox of that period lay in the fact that when Britain's
expanding man-power was at last beginning to enable
her to consider an alternative strategy, her equipment
did not permit her to develop one.

No one makes this clearer than the late Earl Lloyd
George in his Memoirs. In his chapter dealing with the
Munitions Crisis of 1915, the crisis which brought
about the fall of the Liberal Government, and his own
appointment to the newly created Ministry of Munitions, he sets out a remarkable table. This shows that
whereas the Army's main gun, the 18-pounder, re-

quired 50 shells per day per gun to be effective on the Western Front, it was receiving in November 1914 only 9.9 shells per day, and in May 1915 only 11.0. The Army's chief heavy gun, the 4.7, which required 25 shells per day per gun, was obtaining as many as 10.8 in November 1914, but only 4.3 in May 1915. With almost every other munition of war it was a similar story; there were deficiencies in machine-guns, trench mortars, grenades, heavy guns, even rifles. And yet the Gallipoli Campaign was launched, and the strength of other secondary fronts allowed to grow, despite these shortages and the ever-increasing demands of the Army in France. These were two ends that could not meet, and the result, added to a succession of French defeats, was complete frustration for the Allied cause in 1915. By the time, late in 1916, that the British Army could at last deploy its strength with proper equipment, France was no longer able to play her previous part, and Russia was totally expended. The initiative therefore continued to rest with Germany, and did so until her own failures in 1918, coupled with the copious flow of munitions and new weapons that the conditions of the Western Front required, transferred it briefly to the Allies. Reinforced by the Americans, spearheaded by the tanks, this time they made no mistake, and the War ended swiftly when the German Army began to collapse on the front which it had itself made decisive.

In retrospect, it appears that the heat engendered by the long-standing discussions of the merits and opportunities of the several fronts essayed during the First World War, and of others that were never developed, has been largely waste. From the moment, in 1906, when the British Government permitted the British Army to take on the role, if not the status, of a contingent in the French line of battle, it was inevitable that the main strength of the Empire would be deployed in France. From the moment, in 1914, when the Germans relentlessly grasped the initiative, it was inevitable that that strength would have to remain deployed there. Arguments about whether this was the best thing to do, or even a good thing to do, are irrelevant; the enemy was imposing his will, as his first successes permitted him to do. These in short, were the terrible simplicities.

NOTES

1. July 31st, 1914.

2. German troops entered Luxemburg on August 1st.

3. Haldane was Secretary of State for War 1906-1912; his successor, Colonel Seely, resigned in March 1914, after the Curragh incident, whereupon the Prime Minister took over the office.

4, 5, 6. Author's italics.

7. Haig's italics.

8. Largely due to sickness wastage.

The political generation of 1914 seems to tower above most of its predecessors and all of its successors. One contemplates with awe the galaxy which contained, on the Government side, such figures as Haldane, Morley, Asquith himself, Churchill and Lloyd George, and, on the Opposition benches, Balfour, Carson, Curzon and F. E. Smith. To these names were added the special talents of such men as Lord Kitchener and Sir Eric Geddes. The Empire lent its weight to their deliberations: Canada's Borden, Australia's 'Billy' Hughes, New Zealand's Massey, South Africa's Louis Botha and—perhaps most distinguished of all—Jan Smuts. Industrious and resourceful, in the background of all their meetings, conferences and decisions, worked Lord Hankey, who left a mark upon British constitutional practice probably as great as any man's.

It is an ironic reflection that all this talent proved entirely unable to grasp the broad structure of the War, and guide its courses firmly. This was no special British failing: Germany's military autocracy, Russia's despotism, France's Third Republic—all proved equally helpless. On the Allied side, two political figures emerged towards the end who showed at least a greater capacity to dominate than any who had gone before: Clemenceau and Lloyd George. Clemenceau's task was, on the whole, the easier one, for Lloyd George, during all his wartime tenure as Prime Minister, was faced with a terrible dilemma.

LLOYD GEORGE'S DILEMMA

In one of the most percipient passages of his War Memoirs, the late Earl Lloyd George wrote:

'There was an undoubted advantage from the point of view of national unity in having a Liberal rather than a Tory Government in power when war was declared. There was a further advantage in having a Government at the head of affairs which had the support of Labour. . . . But beyond and above all these considerations, as a factor in the attainment of national unity, was the circumstance that the war had been declared by a party which by tradition and training regarded war with the deepest aversion, and had more especially since the days of Gladstone, Cobden and Bright, regarded itself as specially charged with the promotion of the cause of peace.'

In the truths stated there Lloyd George expressed both the strength and weakness of his party as a war-directing agency, and the roots of his own success and failure in the same role. It was only part of the irony of the posture of the Liberal Government in 1914 that, under its aegis, through the indefatigable energy of Lord Haldane, the Army had been brought to its highest pitch of peacetime efficiency in our history. Working swiftly and accurately, Haldane gripped his

problem with a speed that startled and outpaced many
of his colleagues. He was able to present his Bill for
Army Reform as the main plank in the Government's
programme for 1907; his secretary, Sir Gerald Ellison,
wryly commented : 'Radical members were waiting
impatiently for far-reaching measures of social reform,
and pretty disgusted they were to be fobbed off with
a military problem in which they took very little
interest.'

Fortunately, the disinterest of the radicals was not
shared by the Prime Minister, Mr. Asquith. He, for
his part, besides supporting Haldane to the hilt, had
done much to foster and fructify the Committee of
Imperial Defence, created by his Conservative predecessor, Balfour, to study the larger aspects of the
Empire's war policy. But the Liberal Administration
was never able to fuse together the parallel preparations for crisis that it sponsored. Neither Haldane's
new Army, nor his plans for enlarging it, nor the
Navy, were truly fashioned for purposes clearly understood and stated by the Committee of Imperial Defence. There was, in fact, no integrated War Plan.
Consequently, there was no full acceptance of responsibility by the Government as a whole. Despite the fact
that, as one of the members of the Committee wrote,
'no single scheme of attack by us on others was thought
out or prepared', high-minded Liberals were repelled
by the whole subject, and when war broke out two of
them, although deeply implicated in the Committee's
work, resigned—Lord Morley and Mr. Burns. The
point of Lloyd George's observations is clear : had the
Liberals not been in power, how much stronger the

opposition of these men to the War might have been, and how much more support they might have had in the Party, and in the country!

There they were, however, the Liberal Government of 1914, still, with their allies, enjoying a large Parliamentary majority; their edge somewhat blunted by years in office and by the vigour of their programme; distinctly bruised by the intractable Irish problem which had already provided one first-class crisis in 1914; and now faced with the entirely unfamiliar problem of running a European war. The two fundamental issues that faced them were strategy and organisation. Their limitations in respect of both were quickly revealed; the great Council of War summoned by Mr. Asquith on August 5th, 1914, found at once that strategy had been taken out of its hands, while the composition of the Council itself presaged a cumbersome and top-heavy supreme direction of the British war effort.

Indeed, the country had only one set of machinery for conducting its affairs, whether war or peace: the machinery of Parliamentary supremacy, expressed through the collective responsibility of the Cabinet. And at that period—such was the looseness of British constitutional procedure—Cabinet meetings were not minuted; there was no 'follow-through' of any Cabinet decision, beyond the sense of responsibility of individual Ministers; there was not even a precise, 'official' definition of the decisions arrived at. The fact that this system ever worked at all is a remarkable tribute to the innate orderliness of the British character; but even in peacetime, as the volume of Government business expanded to meet modern situations, defects had become apparent. With the outbreak of war, the whole apparatus became obsolete. Writing of the year 1917, the critical turning-point of the War, Sir Edward Spears has said : 'The old coat of democracy, never intended for wear at Armageddon, was showing white at the seams.' In truth, the seams began to burst the moment war was declared.

The War lost no time in declaring its nature : it was a national struggle. Gone were the days when two professional Services could be relied upon to deal with the country's enemies, at the price of a little civilian discomfort, somewhat higher taxation, and a few tremors on the Stock Exchange. Now, in 1914, Government was called upon to do two things : to regulate the military policy of the nation, and to mobilise its entire resources behind that policy. The harsh truth is that it was too late for either purpose to wait until war had been declared. The Liberal failure to grasp the meaning of the Entente Cordiale, to appreciate the implications of the Staff talks between Britain and France that had begun as early as 1906, and which had decided the character and purpose of the Army that Haldane created, largely robbed the Government of strategic initiative when war broke out, just as the French failure to penetrate the quality of German preparations robbed the Allied cause as a whole of that same initiative. For that reason the British effort throughout the War took on the appearance of improvisation, of being perpetually surprised, or perpetually ramming at a brick wall.

This, of course, was an intolerable situation for intelligent men, and so a pattern gradually imposed itself of distrust and conflict between the Service leaders who, willy-nilly, had to grapple from day to day with things as they were, and those who, recognising that matters were in a lamentable state, were trying from day to day to transform them into something else. This conflict lay at the root of the organisational problem; for, as the War continued, it became apparent that much of the internal confusion might have been more quickly and easily resolved if Ministers had had more confidence that the resources they were expected to mobilise would be correctly applied. To no Minister was this more applicable than to Mr. Lloyd George.

It is not without significance that the first alteration in the constitutional machinery for the direction of the War was linked with the only attempt made to create an alternative British strategy, which would free the main effort of the country from the mire of the Western Front, and bring sea-power into play. At the end of November 1914, when the opposing lines in the West had settled down into the positions that they were to occupy with only minor changes for the rest of the War, a number of people arrived at the conclusion that an impasse had been reached, and that a way round the German fortified line must be found.

Mr. Winston Churchill, the First Lord of the Admiralty, was naturally not without ideas on this subject; nor was he backward in bringing them to the Prime Minister's attention. To consider the projects advanced by his young and thrustful colleague, Asquith decided that a committee of the Cabinet would be more appropriate than the full Cabinet itself,

with its upward of twenty members. He therefore set
up what was called for a time the War Council.
This body, with no fixed composition or constitution,
meeting at irregular intervals, became the legislative
and executive arm of the Cabinet for all purposes connected with the higher direction of the War. Being
smaller, it was an improvement on the full Cabinet
(though at times it was not that much smaller); it was a
step towards something new that was badly needed;
but its limitation was apparent in the very manner of
its birth. The only strategic subject that it could usefully discuss was, as it turned out, the Dardanelles
Expedition. After six months, it changed its name, and
called itself frankly the Dardanelles Committee.

It is worth pausing here for a moment, to examine
why it came about that the body charged most immediately with the supreme direction of the British
Empire's war effort at the end of almost a year's
fighting should be named after one in particular out
of many theatres of war, and a minor one at that. The
answer is not difficult to find, but it illuminates the
constant frustrations both of that Committee and of its
successors. The point was that the Dardanelles Campaign was the one and only exercise of British amphibious initiative, the only area with a promise of more
than local victory where Great Britain's attributes
would enable her to play a decisive part. All other
subjects, other than purely naval or imperial, no
matter how deeply one might think about them, discuss them, and take 'decisions' about them, were in
fact decided elsewhere than in London by two im-
mutable factors : the exigencies of the French Alliance,

and the initiative seized by Germany in 1914.

No one has expressed the pathetic plight of British statesmen at that time better than Churchill. He refers bitterly to a conference held at Calais in July 1915, at which the British representatives, Asquith, Balfour and Kitchener, urged on the French that further offensives should not be undertaken by the Allies on the Western Front during that year.

> 'The French had agreed; General Joffre had agreed. The agreement was open and formal. And it was on this basis that we had looked forward and prepared for the new battle on the Gallipoli Peninsula. No sooner, however, had General Joffre left the Conference than, notwithstanding these agreements, he had calmly resumed the development of his plans for his great attack in Champagne, in which he confidently expected to break the German lines and roll them back. It was not until after the Battle of Suvla Bay had been finally lost, and we were more deeply committed in the Peninsula than ever before, that we became aware of this.'

The point is not that Joffre's attack 'spoilt' the British effort at Gallipoli; it did not. That effort failed for reasons of its own, as Joffre's did too. The point is that the British Prime Minister and his most eminent colleagues were unable to impose any kind of restraint on the French Commander-in-Chief. The entire episode shows how unrealistic have been all subsequent speculations on what Britain 'should have' or 'should not have' done in 1915. Britain had to do pretty well what the French decided, for naturally Joffre's plans included participation by the British in the West on the largest scale possible; and the French, as I have said once before, were dancing to the German tune in that year and the next.

By the end of 1916, when Mr. Lloyd George became Prime Minister, the outlook from his point of view—and he was the leader of those statesmen and some few soldiers who felt particularly depressed by the course the War had taken—seemed thoroughly black. After France's heavy losses in 1915, and the terrible strain that the Germans had inflicted upon her at Verdun at the beginning of the new year, the British Army had been forced, before it was really ready, to assume the main role in the West. The result had been the Battle of the Somme, with its 415,000 British casualties and the virtual destruction of Kitchener's volunteer armies, for the gain of a very narrow strip indeed of muddy ground in Picardy. The battle, with all its terrifying consumption of human life and laboriously produced war matériel, had not prevented the Germans from detaching sufficient strength to crush Roumania almost as soon as she had thrown in her lot with the Allies. The Russians, despite a brilliant offensive under General Brusiloff, were now evidently very much weakened. Italy had done nothing of note. France was palpably nearing exhaustion. The Grand Fleet had not come well out of Jutland. The menace of the submarines was assuming the most alarming shape. The only consolation was that General Joffre, who had loomed over the whole Allied effort, massive, obstinate and omnipotent until now, had gone at last. And in England, Lloyd George had made it his immediate business to streamline the machinery of war direction by the institution of a compact War Cabinet of seven members, with a proper system of minutes and circulars organised by Colonel Hankey. This at least promised that things might now at last get done. But what?

From the moment of his accession to power until the War ended, this was to be Lloyd George's great problem, and the one that, with all his attributes, his fire, his imagination, his driving energy, his impatience of red tape, his capacity to 'think big', and his indomitable will to victory, he was least able to solve. By the time he became Prime Minister, he had reached certain conclusions about the military conduct of the War, and his tenure of office during it was guided by these conclusions. He had witnessed with growing horror the seemingly endless and pointless slaughter on the Western Front. He had seen the British endeavours at Neuve Chapelle splutter out like a damp cracker; at Aubers, founder in the mud; at Loos, collapse through incompetence on the part of the Commander-in-Chief which he secretly felt was shared by a number of other senior commanders; on the Somme, grind forward yard by bloody yard until the butcher's bill surpassed any nightmare. And what did the soldiers now propose? They proposed to go on in the same way, to do the same things all over again, to cause the deaths of more hundreds of thousands of men, until finally, they claimed, Germany would collapse through this attrition. The prospect revolted him. Conscious of the swelling might of Britain and her Empire, he could not abide the thought that it must all be expended in this gross and brutal manner.

In all war situations, behind the theories, behind the weapons, stand the men. What now presented itself to Lloyd George was a clash of personalities more drastic and more fraught with terrible consequences than any he had yet experienced. He was now dealing directly with a kind of man with whom he was entirely unfamiliar; the professional soldier of top calibre. This was something very different from even his most deter-mined Tory opponents in the House of Commons or the House of Lords. This was a type of person with whom he had no affinities at all, and with whom his relationship must begin on the basis of profound mutual antipathy. For his own Liberal distrust of all things military was matched by their innate loathing of the whole genus 'politician', of which he was all too evidently a particularly dangerous specimen.[1]

Communication was clearly going to be a major problem, and it was bad luck for both parties that the two soldiers with whom Lloyd George would have chiefly to deal were both men who found communication extremely difficult, except in the manner that he found most indigestible. Both the Chief of the Imperial General Staff, Sir William Robertson, and the Commander-in-Chief of the British Expeditionary Force, Sir Douglas Haig, were men who, except among their intimates, had the greatest difficulty in putting their thoughts into words; but both could achieve, on paper, with astonishing regularity and ease, a lucidity and logic which, while entirely satisfying to the authors, could only enrage a mind like Lloyd George's, working mainly through feeling and imagination.

This inability to exchange ideas was fundamental. It had the worst possible effect at the time, and even now it can be most confusing to the student, who finds the two parties to the same dispute speaking and writing of it almost as though in different tongues, so separate are their views of the same events. In a revealing passage, Lloyd George showed his own consciousness of this perpetual obstacle. 'Haig', he wrote in his War Memoirs, 'was devoid of the gift of intelligible and coherent expression. Fluency is not a proof—nor a disproof—of ability, but lucidity of speech is unquestionably one of the surest tests of mental precision. . . . Lucidity of mind ensures lucidity of expression. Power and light go together and are generated by the same machine. Mere slowness of mind is no evidence of mental deficiency except where quick decisions are essential to effective action. I have known men of sluggish mentality, who, given time, were very sound thinkers. So I have met men of slow speech who were clear expositors. But in my experience a confused talker is never a clear thinker.' This is a very characteristic piece of Lloyd George; he had no consciousness, in writing this, that he was exposing a weakness. But his son has given us a vignette of this theory in action; he has described a meeting between his father and Haig at which he was present:

'Father was trying to explain some particular question about the disposition of reserves, and the arguments were presented from every possible angle to convey comprehension. To say that four times three made twelve would not be enough; one had to add that this was because we had already established that three times four make twelve, too. Haig's part in the conversation consisted of a series of grunts, monosyllables, raised eyebrows and scowls.'

If the setting were not so tragic, one could laugh at the picture. It is not hard to imagine the passionate loquacity with which Lloyd George would broach to Haig a 'particular question about the disposition of reserves', the House of Commons eloquence with which he would seek to instruct the soldier in his own professional arts. And it is not hard to imagine the words that would fail Haig. There is, of course, another method of conversing with men like Haig; but it presupposes a little humility, and a little respect. J. A. Spender has left us with this example :

'I have a memory of Haldane in respectful talk with a tongue-tied, verbally incoherent, but extremely able soldier. How patiently he worked at him, how skilfully he brought up the buried treasure without breaking any of it, with what goodwill they parted, and what mutual desire to meet again ! Haldane was in all these respects an extraordinarily modest man, and entirely free from that worst vice of politicians of putting the dialectically unaccomplished in the wrong when they are essentially in the right. He knew the value of the able inarticulate and could never be imposed upon by voluble superficiality.'

These, then, were the auspices under which Lloyd George approached his heavy task, as the fatal year

1917 began. The two men through whom he would
have mostly to work for victory were men with whom
he could not communicate—for what was true of Haig
was true of Robertson, but worse, because Robertson
was in Whitehall. And both these men were profoundly
convinced of one thing—that the decisive theatre of
operations, despite all the disappointments associated
with it, was the Western Front.

This is not the occasion to discuss the pros and cons
of 'Western' versus 'Eastern' strategy. The point of
view both of the General Staff at the War Office and
of G.H.Q. in France may be summed up in Robertson's words:

> 'An essential condition of success in war being the
> concentration of effort on the "decisive front", or
> place where the main issue will probably be fought
> out, it follows that soldiers and statesmen charged
> with the direction of military operations should be
> agreed amongst themselves as to where that front
> is. Should any difference of opinion exist—as it
> usually will, sooner or later—it must be thrashed out
> and a definite conclusion reached, *and this must be
> honestly and completely accepted by all concerned.*[2]
> If these precautions are not taken, the operations
> will be of the nature of half-measures and compro-
> mise, and may indeed end in disaster. . . . In the
> Great War the decisive front was fixed for us by the
> deployment of the enemy's masses in France and
> Belgium . . .'

To this the General Staff would add that the possession of the interior lines by the Central Powers

enabled them to move more easily to meet any Allied threat than the Allies could mount such a threat. This summed up the basic reasoning of the best qualified soldiers in the Army. Little joy had they had from it, up to the beginning of 1917; but as that year dawned, they saw one gleam of light at least on the horizon. The growing weakness of France, and the fall of Joffre, at last suggested an opportunity for Great Britain to take the lead in military matters to which soldiers and many politicians alike felt that her growing resources and undiminished fighting quality entitled her. As Lloyd George rightly said : 'The British Army was the one allied army in the field which could be absolutely depended on for any enterprise.'

Leaving aside now the rights and wrongs of the two strategic schools, we find an extraordinary situation at the beginning of 1917 : for his accession to chief office coincided with Lloyd George's one brief, painful espousal of 'Westernism'. The tragedy was that, in adopting the orientation of his responsible military advisers, he was actually trying to relegate and diminish them. For the man who won him over to belief in a quick, cheap, victory on the Western Front was neither Haig nor Robertson, nor any other British officer, but Joffre's successor, General Nivelle. Nivelle was sure that he had a formula for breaking through the German lines, rolling them up and flinging them back, in forty-eight hours of violent battle. He also believed that, if he did not succeed, he would be able to break off the battle at the end of that time. There would be 'no more Sommes'. This tempting theory, expressed with an eloquence all too rare in the soldiers of the day, in fluent English (an unknown tongue to most French generals), by a man with considerable personal charm, completely won over Lloyd George. He was all the more impressed because his interest in phrenology persuaded him that the bumps on Nivelle's head were deserving of every confidence. Here, at last, was the 'Napoleonic' genius who had been so conspicuously lacking throughout the War—or so it seemed.

From Lloyd George's hasty conversion the direst results were to flow. He decided that the British effort, and the British commanders, must be subordinated to this glittering new French strategy. There followed the amazing incident of the Calais Conference on February 26th, 1917. After consultations with the French, which he kept secret from his War Cabinet colleagues and the C.I.G.S., Lloyd George used this meeting between the civil and military heads of Britain and France, ostensibly convened to discuss a grave transport crisis, as an opening for Nivelle to put forward proposals which would have reduced the forces of the British Empire in France to a mere contingent in the French Army, and reduced the British Commander-in-Chief to a glorified Adjutant-General. Haig and Robertson were stunned and outraged. The new French Minister of War, Lyautey, was horrified when he saw that the British Prime Minister was contemplating such a change in direct opposition to his two leading soldiers. Briand, the French Prime Minister, who had certainly not been unaware of what was afoot, and Nivelle, who had arrived at the Conference with his proposals remarkably cut and dried, both per-

ceived that they had somewhat over-played their hand.
On the British side, fortunately, Colonel (later Lord)
Hankey was present, to find a way out of the impossible situation. He devised a formula whereby Haig's
subordination to Nivelle would only be for the period
of the forthcoming great attack; and to this, unwil-
lingly, Haig and Robertson appended their signatures.
Both later regretted that they had done so; neither ever
really trusted Lloyd George again.

The sequel was ironic. Within a matter of weeks, the
Germans completed their withdrawal to the Hindenburg Line, an act which the British General Staff interpreted as a vindication of the British fighting on the
Somme, since it clearly implied a refusal by the enemy
to stand and fight the British on that ground, in that
way, again. But if the withdrawal paid tribute to
British success in 1916, it largely frustrated French success in 1917, by robbing Nivelle of half of his front of
attack. Rapidly he lost the support of his senior Army
Group commanders, Micheler and Pétain; not long
afterwards, he lost the support of his Government, too.
And the ludicrous position was arrived at where the
British Army was actually under the command of a
French general whom his own Government did not
trust.

Nivelle's offensive, when it came, though not unsuccessful nor over-expensive by contemporary stan-
dards, fell so far short of what he had promised, and
revealed such organisational defects, that it brought
about his immediate disgrace, and shortly afterwards
widespread mutinies in the French Army. So ended
Lloyd George's first attempt to override the policy of

the British General Staff. The only successful part in the whole proceedings was that played by Haig's army, in its supporting role at Arras, which included the brilliant capture of the Vimy Ridge. For a short time Lloyd George was prepared to admit openly that there might be some good in British generals after all; and he even went so far as to say that he gave them a free hand.

This honeymoon did not last long. As preparations reached completion for the main British effort of the year in Flanders, the Prime Minister's misgivings mounted again. As the Flanders attack, the Third Battle of Ypres, usually but misleadingly known as Passchendaele, wallowed forward laboriously in the mud of one of the wettest summers and most dismal autumns in that region, Lloyd George began to cast around for a new expedient by which he could rid himself of the burden of this bloody and apparently unproductive strategy. Since subordination of the British to the French had been tried and found wanting, under the active stimulus of Sir Henry Wilson, then currently unemployed, he began to think in terms of a supreme authority that would regulate the plans and endeavours of all the Allies.

This concept came to fruition in November, at Rapallo, where the Supreme War Council was born. Britain, France, Italy and, later, America, agreed to accept this body as the central deciding authority on their military policy, and the allocation of their resources; each country was represented by a civilian Head of Mission, with a military Technical Adviser. In theory, it was a sensible move towards unity of

council and action; in practice, the whole organisation, with the large staffs that were found necessary for
its functioning, was too cumbersome for use, and too
much at the mercy of the frequently conflicting
interests of the Powers that composed it. From the
British point of view, it had yet another disadvantage :
the soldier selected to be the British Technical Adviser,
and thereby in theory to have the decisive say for
Britain on strategy, was Sir Henry Wilson, chosen
because Lloyd George believed him to be opposed to
the views of the British Government's responsible adviser, Robertson. In fact, the whole machinery was
simply yet another device for by-passing and overruling Haig and Robertson. But no other Power was
prepared to use the Supreme War Council for such a
purpose; the soldiers representing France, Italy and
America were all either the Chiefs of Staff of those
countries or their spokesmen. As his biographer remarked, 'Wilson's position was, in fact, going to be the
exceptional one . . .' And so, once more, at a juncture
when the voice of Britain should have been heard with
greater attention than ever, and should have held
greater authority in Allied councils, it was weakened
by division; and relations between the Government
and its military chiefs, already poisoned at Calais,
suffered another relapse.

It was not long, however, before this device, and
much else besides, was put to the supreme test of
battle. As German preparations for a new offensive in
the West, with the troops released by the collapse of
Russia, became more evident, the weakness of the
Supreme War Council was exposed. Its only possibility

of exercising any decisive influence over the coming battle lay in the formation and handling of a strategic Reserve; but neither Haig nor Pétain was prepared to part with any troops whatever to compose this Reserve. Both generals preferred to rely on mutual arrangements with each other, rather than on the chancy workings of a distant committee. Wilson warned Haig that 'he would have to live on Pétain's charity, and he would find that very cold charity. But I was quite unable to persuade him . . .' Wilson was right about this; but in other respects his views were less clear than they had been; indeed, they were changing sharply. For he had now become C.I.G.S., with the resignation of Robertson at last; and, as C.I.G.S., Henry Wilson found that the independent position on which he had insisted for the British representative on the Supreme War Council was not such a good thing after all. He now demanded that the officer there must be junior to him; 'the whole thing', he complained to his diary, 'is rather muddlesome'. It was also rather academic; for when the German blow fell on March 21st, 1918, it was quickly seen that neither the Supreme War Council nor any other part of existing Allied arrangements was capable of meeting the final crisis.

The day of decision was March 24th; and the onus of decision fell, as one might expect, on the commander in the field, Sir Douglas Haig. On that day he discovered to his horror that Pétain was not prepared to put all his strength into preserving the link between the British and French armies in front of Amiens; he was contemplating falling back to cover Paris, while the British fell back on their bases, the Channel Ports. Haig at once perceived the terrible danger, and the only way out of it; he wired instantly to London for the C.I.G.S. and a Government representative to come out and appoint Foch as Generalissimo, with power to overrule Pétain. He named Foch, not because of any inflated idea of that general's professional skill, but because he knew him to be outstanding among the French officers for indomitable courage and tenacity. And thus, by particular irony, it came about that the supreme direction of the Allied war effort that Lloyd George had been trying in so many devious ways to establish was actually achieved by Haig. 'I can deal with a man,' he said, 'but not with a committee.' For the remainder of the War he and Foch dealt together on the terms of mutual respect created by their long association in battle; as Haig's armies, later in the year, passed to the offensive, and became the spear-head of the Allied advance, his influence on Foch increased, and on more than one critical occasion guided the latter's plans along the course that produced victory in 1918.

Naturally, Lloyd George claimed much credit for the outcome of events; because he had fought continuously for some kind of superior direction of the Allied cause, he tended to attribute the final victory to that factor. He preferred to gloss over the fact that the superior direction, when it came, arrived in a manner which he had not anticipated, and was exercised by two men whose strategic ideas he had always bitterly opposed. Because of the success of the Supreme Commander principle in the Second World War, a subsequent generation has been disposed to take a similar view. The truth is not quite so simple. Nothing could be more misleading than to liken the command exercised by Foch, which was essentially a personal leadership in the field, to that exercised by Eisenhower, which was based on a fusion of staffs and methods that was never attainable in 1918. But out of all the tribulations of that year, and the gloomy experiences that preceded it, one truth became apparent in quarters where it could do most good : whatever the disagreements, whatever the strains, Winston Churchill had learned that a Government can only make war through its responsible advisers; when his turn came, he never overruled them; he never went behind their backs. He was prepared to change them, as he was entitled to do; and this was the one way out of his dilemma that Lloyd George was not bold enough to take. And that, one may say, was just as well; but the cost of compromise was terribly high.

NOTES

1. Why, one wonders, did soldiers have this almost pathological dislike of politicians of all Parties? Probably because they saw the 'frocks' simply as the men who habitually slashed the Army Estimates, and still expected the soldiers to win wars for them.

2. Author's italics.

It is impossible to understand Britain's role during the last years of the War without also understanding Lloyd George's point of view, the passion with which he held it, and the depth of the gulf which separated him from the military leaders. Constantly, in studying the War, I have found myself returning to this bitter and tragic struggle of personalities and ideas. It overhung the entire period containing such sombre names in the British Army's history as Arras, Passchendaele, Cambrai, the 'March Offensive' and the Battle of the Lys. Because of the bitterness of the dispute, when the tide turned, and the British Army, under Haig, won that series of unparalleled victories which did so much to hasten the end of the War, Lloyd George could never bring himself to admit what had been achieved. The most that he offered, by way of credit, was the statement that Haig 'did well in the concluding stages of the 1918 campaign—under Foch's supreme direction'. How well he did, we shall see in a later essay; meanwhile we need to pay somewhat closer attention to the events which the immediately preceding article has lightly sketched. For the manner in which Lloyd George pursued his policies was as dangerously productive of mistrust as any defect in the policies themselves. Eighteen decisive months of war were clouded and obstructed by Lloyd George's expedients.

LLOYD GEORGE'S EXPEDIENTS
PART I

The winter of 1916-1917 was one of the severest in modern European experience. A Brigadier-General serving in France recorded : 'Never was there a winter such as the men endured in 1916 and 1917.' In London Colonel Repington wrote on January 31st, 1917 : 'The cold continues : the hardest winter I remember since 1880-'81.' These conditions persisted well into April; on the 16th of that month, when General Nivelle launched his great offensive along the normally sheltered valley of the Aisne, the French troops attacked through blinding sleet and snow. Summer came late and vanished swiftly; it was a bleak year, glacial alike to men's senses and their hopes.

For the British people, the turning of the year held a special significance, as depressing as the weather : it marked their first full recognition of the meaning of total war. In 1916 they had witnessed the crumbling of the force on which their pre-eminence had rested for centuries—the supremacy of the Royal Navy.

The failure of the attempt at a naval strategy implicit in the Gallipoli campaign had been followed by the disappointing performance of the Grand Fleet at Jutland, and then by the growth of a menace that the Navy seemed helpless to avert. Unrestricted submarine warfare inflicted, during the last four months of 1916, a loss of 632,000 tons gross of British shipping. 'At the end of 1916', wrote Lloyd George, 'we were short (as our shipping was then handled) of well over 50 per cent of the tonnage required for imports of what the President of the Board of Trade reckoned to be our irreducible needs.' To this threat, the Admiralty told the Government: 'No conclusive answer has as yet been found . . . perhaps no conclusive answer ever will be found.'

Nothing was more calculated to bring home the true meaning of war to an island race which had hitherto sought to conduct military affairs on the principle of 'limited liability'. The reluctance of people and leaders alike to face the full implications of their situation is well expressed in a speech made by Walter Runciman in the House of Commons as late as October 17th, 1916. He said :

'. . . The one thing that we ought to avoid in this country is, from any cause whatever, to put ourselves in the position of a blockaded people. Bread tickets, meat coupons, all these artificial arrangements are harmful, and they are harmful to those who have the least with which to buy. . . . We want to avoid any rationing of our people in food.'

This was a vain hope. One month later, a new series of regulations authorised the Board of Trade to impose drastic restrictions upon food consumption. In January 1917, a first batch of six orders detailed the nature of these restrictions; in February, the Government appealed for voluntary rationing; in March and April, as the submarine menace swelled, this was converted into full control, largely completed by May. Even with these measures, by December 1917, food queues had become such an alarming feature of the national life that special steps had to be taken to reorganise distribution.

It was against this gloomy background that Lloyd George became Prime Minister in place of Asquith on December 7th, 1916. It is not to be wondered at that the new Premier was deeply conscious of the nation's misgivings, or that his policies should be framed in their light. There was little comfort to him, moreover, in the apparent posture of the vast land forces, some four and a half million men, which completed the picture of the British war effort. Progress in the secondary theatres of the War, Salonika, Egypt, Mesopotamia and East Africa, continued to be disappointingly slow. In the main theatre , France and Flanders, where over one and a half million men were deployed, it appeared to Lloyd George that not only was no progress being made, but that the cost of attempting it was prohibitively and disgracefully high. The long-drawn-out Battle of the Somme had ended in a wasteland of mud in November 1916. At a cost of 415,000 casualties, in a series of conflicts of a ferocity never before envisaged, the British had inched their way forward over a narrow strip of territory, falling short of many of the objectives they had set themselves for the *first day* of the offensive.

The High Command was not dissatisfied with this result, recognising the irreparable damage that had been done to the German Army (openly acknowledged when the Germans fell back to the Hindenburg Line rather than undergo another similar experience). But to Lloyd George this attitude spelt the worst kind of unimaginative complacency. On October 25th, 1916, he told Repington '. . . that we were all asked to keep silent and bow the knee to this military Moloch, but that he was responsible,[1] and as he would have to take the blame, he meant to have his own way . . .' A week later he told Colonel Hankey he 'considered that the Somme offensive had been a bloody and disastrous failure; he was not willing to remain in office if it was to be repeated next year . . .' This was a frame of mind that persisted and grew upon him, so that in February he was saying that he was 'not prepared to accept the position of a butcher's boy driving cattle to the slaughter, and that he would not do it'. For the remainder of the War he clung to this idea; like many humanitarian ideals, its working out in practice was accompanied by widespread suffering and dreadful loss of life.

It was, then, with these apprehensions that he viewed plans agreed by the Allied military leaders for the year 1917, and it is because of them that he grasped so eagerly at whatever alternative offered itself. Inter-Allied plans had been formulated at the Chantilly Conference of November 15th and 16th, 1916, at which both Lloyd George and Asquith were present. With the full agreement of the British, Belgian, Russian, Italian, Japanese, Roumanian and Serbian representatives, the French proposals, put forward by General Joffre, were accepted. These were based on the concept, agreed a year before but scarcely realised during 1916, of simultaneous attacks by all the Allies together on the citadel of the Central Powers. Pressure would be maintained during the winter as far as climatic conditions permitted; at the earliest opportunity in the spring (Joffre urged February, Haig preferred to wait until May) all-out offensives on *all fronts* would seek the decision prepared by the 'wearing-out battles' of 1916. 'Final victory cannot be obtained by a slow indefinite attrition of the adverse forces . . .' said Joffre. For 1917 something else was necessary : a co-ordinated knock-out blow, the main weight of which would be delivered in the West.

But Joffre's days were numbered. His great name was now tarnished by the memory of costly and unsuccessful offensives in 1915, and above all by the dreadful blood-letting of Verdun, followed by a further large French effort (195,000 casualties) on the Somme. At the end of December Joffre was replaced by General Robert Nivelle, who brought with him to high office a brand-new plan for finishing off the War by one swift blow in a matter of forty-eight hours. Disliking Joffre's plans more the more he contemplated them, and disappointed at the rejection of his own schemes for making Italy the decisive theatre, Lloyd George grasped eagerly at this specious elixir. Not the least of its attractions for him was the opportunity it offered of setting aside and overruling the two British soldiers whom Lloyd George most disliked and distrusted : Field-Marshal Sir Douglas Haig, the Commander-in-Chief of the British Expeditionary Force, and General Sir William Robertson, the Chief of the Imperial General Staff.

Already these two were preparing their offensive

plans for 1917, pursuant to British Government instructions and the decisions of the Chantilly Conference. Asquith had handed an unsigned note to Robertson in November 1916 which said : 'There is no
operation of war to which the War Committee would
attach greater importance than the successful occupation . . . of Ostend, and especially Zeebrugge.'² Haig
had received from Joffre on December 10th a plan
of operations whose 'objective is the capture of the
Belgian coast by a combined operation of British Army
and Fleet, French and Belgians, all to be under a
British General. This is practically the scheme at which
I have aimed for the past twelve months. . . . My
difficulty, however, was to get the French C.-in-C. to
view the situation in the same light as I do. Now this
has been achieved, the rest of the preliminary arrangements can be proceeded with at once.' This endeavour
would clearly be the main British contribution to the
year's fighting, and even without his subsequent after-
knowledge of the hell of 'Passchendaele', Lloyd George
was able to detect a whiff of another 'Somme'.

Nivelle's plan was quite different. Founded on the
concept of one mighty blow, which would necessarily
have to be delivered by a homogeneous army (i.e. the
French), it reduced the British role to a subsidiary one.
This was entirely pleasing to Lloyd George, promising
freedom from the otherwise insoluble problems of
man-power that haunted him until the end of the
War, and promising too, if Nivelle was successful, the
liberation of the Belgian coast on which his naval
advisers insisted. In other words, here, it seemed, was a
chance of winning 'on the cheap', a temptation that

few politicians can resist, despite the lessons of history. Lloyd George gave Nivelle his full approval. He went further : he handed Robertson a 'special instruction' for Haig, insisting that the British should carry out their part of Nivelle's plan 'in the letter and in the spirit', and added : 'On no account must the French have to wait for us owing to our arrangements not being complete.' For the time being Lloyd George's conversion to the strategy of 'Westernism' was more complete and sanguine than that of the soldiers whom he so suspected.

What he need not have suspected was Haig's loyalty to agreements once reached with his Allies. 'We must do our utmost to help the French to make their effort a success,' he was telling his Chief of Staff. 'If they succeed, we also benefit. If they fail . . . we then have a right to expect their full support to enable us to launch our decisive attack . . .' But loyal support is not the same as complete conviction; neither Haig nor Robertson (nor, for that matter, many leading French generals) was fully convinced by Nivelle's promises. Robertson warned the War Cabinet 'that it is possible that Nivelle may not be able to do all that he now thinks and says he can accomplish. In that case we must work out our Northern scheme of operations. We must now make our plans accordingly.'[3] These sober considerations alarmed Lloyd George; he detected in them an attempt to by-pass the Nivelle Plan; they helped to determine him upon a remarkable course of action.

Haig's problems were now acute. He was committed to help Nivelle with a large diversionary operation at

Arras, timed to precede Nivelle's own attack, requiring a considerable build-up of munitions and material. He was also conscious of the need to maintain his preliminary preparations in Flanders, in case Nivelle should fail, and an attack be required there after all. This, too, made its logistical demands. And to cap everything, under the stress of this abominable winter, the Nord Railway system now threatened to break down. Nivelle at first appeared to believe that this factor was not real, but was merely being used as an excuse by Haig to delay and diminish participation in the great attack. A *'most* satisfactory' discussion between them on February 16th disposed of Nivelle's doubts: 'He at once sent a stiff wire to the French Government recommending that the Nord Railway Co. be placed on a sound footing at once.' Accord was re-established, but fatal damage had been done. Lloyd George seized upon the transport crisis as an opportunity to settle once and for all with his recalcitrant soldiers.

On the very day that Haig and Nivelle were reaching agreement about the condition of the Nord Railway, Commandant Bertier de Sauvigny, the French Liaison Officer at the War Office, reported to his Government and to Nivelle an extraordinary conversation in which he had taken part the day before. He had been talking to Colonel Hankey,[4] when they were interrupted by Mr. Lloyd George. The Prime Minister told Bertier of the good impression that General Nivelle had made on the British War Cabinet; Bertier continues:

' "For my part," he said to me, "I have complete

confidence in him, and the deepest conviction that he is the only man who is capable of bringing the operations to a successful conclusion this year. But, for this to be possible, it is necessary in the last resort that he should be able to make use of all the forces on the French front, ours as well as the French Armies." Mr. Lloyd George is making every effort to bring his colleagues round to this point of view, but does not count on being successful, unless Nivelle and the French Government take up a strong line on the subject. "There is no doubt that the prestige which Field-Marshal Haig enjoys with the public and the British Army will make it impossible to subordinate him purely and simply to the French Command, but if the War Cabinet realises that this measure is indispensable they will not hesitate to give Field-Marshal Haig secret instructions to this effect; and, if need be, to replace him if he will not give the support of all his forces when this may be required, with complete understanding and compliance. It is essential that the War Cabinets should be in agreement on this principle. A conference should be held as soon as possible, for although the date by which the British Armies will be ready has been retarded by a fortnight owing to the congestion of the French railways, it is nevertheless so near that we must take a decision as soon as possible. I should like, therefore, to fix this interview for February 28th." '

'The War Cabinet', added Bertier, 'intends to unmask its batteries against Haig's plans.' This was incorrect; it was not the War Cabinet that was opposed to 'Haig's plans', it was Lloyd George, who had recognised a brilliant chance of reducing Haig's status. It seemed that he could not fail : either Haig would become merely a subordinate of the French C.-in-C., or, better still, faced with such a prospect he might well resign. The only problem was to win the War Cabinet approval that Bertier was taking for granted, and this might prove difficult at a time when people in England were increasingly demanding that Britain's voice should be asserted more firmly in the alliance, rather than less. One of the most vociferous of these advocates was Robertson; for that reason (and there would be others) it was scarcely likely that Lloyd George would have his way unless he took special measures. The War Cabinet met on February 24th; Robertson tells us :

'The Secretary to the War Cabinet, acting presumably on the Prime Minister's instructions, had telephoned to me to say that unless I had any special question to bring forward I need not attend the Cabinet meeting that day—a very unusual occurrence. Having none, I did not attend, and had no reason to suppose that any question connected with the coming conference would be considered.'

This stratagem disposed of Robertson; but Lloyd George knew quite well that, even in the absence of that redoubtable figure, the War Cabinet would be unlikely to digest the diet he had to offer : the simple subordination of the great British Citizen Army in France, with its large Dominion contingents, to the

T.W.F.—D

French High Command. Another stratagem was needed; the nature of it we learn from Lord Derby (Secretary of State for War):

> 'Mr. Lloyd George told us at the War Cabinet that, although an agreement had been arrived at at the Conference in London, there was nothing to which both our own representatives and those of the French had put their hand in a formal signature, and it was very advisable, in view of possible recriminations afterwards, to get those signatures. I therefore was under the impression that this was the sole object of the Conference so far as the fresh offensive was concerned, but that the matter of transportation was also going to be discussed.'[5]

Thus the stage was cleared, and the plot prepared; as Sir Edward Spears has said: 'General Robertson and Sir Douglas Haig were to be taken by surprise. The method employed makes one think of latter-day American gangsters. They were to be "taken for a ride" to Calais, and there "put on the spot".'

The conference was held on February 26th, and Calais was the venue. From London came Lloyd George and Hankey, with Robertson and his assistant, General Maurice. From G.H.Q. came Haig and (later) his Chief of Staff, General Kiggell, with (at Haig's suggestion, this being ostensibly a Transport conference) General Geddes, the Director-General of Transportation. From Paris came the French Prime Minister, M. Briand, the War Minister, General Lyautey, Nivelle, and two leading French railway experts, M. Claveille and General Ragenau. The London party

arrived at lunchtime, 1.15 p.m., and at that meal Haig
sat next to Lloyd George; he suggested to the Prime
Minister that they should have a quarter of an hour
together (with Geddes) before the formal conference
opened. To this Lloyd George agreed, but no sooner
was lunch finished than he hurried away to confer
privately with Briand, shortly afterwards sending word
that he would go straight to the conference without
meeting Haig and Geddes first. This was an irritant,
but insufficient in itself to arouse suspicion.

When the conference opened at 3.30 p.m., 'transport occupied much of our time'—according to Lloyd
George. This impression is his alone; 'the proceedings
in regard to transportation occupied a very short time',
says Robertson; more specifically, Haig noted: 'The
Conference on Transportation thus broke up after
sitting for barely an hour.' Inevitably, as the experts
unfolded their views, this railway discussion became
complex and detailed, and we need not question the
soldiers' version. Haig tells us that Lloyd George 'broke
in' on the technicalities 'and said that he thought it
would be better if the railway specialists withdrew and
settled their differences together, whilst the more important question of "Plans" was dealt with at once.
For me this was quite a new and unexpected development. But doubtless this had all been planned by L.G.
with Briand beforehand.[6] 'The absence after lunch was
now accounted for. The railway experts went away :
the first part of the conference was over, and its true
meaning about to emerge. Meanwhile, there was a
short break for tea.

When the reduced delegations reconvened, Lloyd

George at once called upon General Nivelle to speak. One senses that the French commander did so with some diffidence, despite careful priming; he outlined once again his famous plan (using a map)—familiar ground to all present—and made agreeable references to the 'accord' which existed between him and Haig. Agreeable, that is to say, except to Lloyd George, who, when Nivelle asked for questions, 'said "that is not all —I want to hear everything", and to Briand he said, "Tell him to keep nothing back" and so forth, "as to his disagreements with Marshal Haig". This was quite a surprise to me, and apparently to Nivelle to some extent.'

What now followed, to Lloyd George's disgust, was another technical discussion, this time in military terms, a debate about tactics between Haig and Nivelle. Haig had already paid a compliment to the friendly relations between the two General Head-quarters, and now added 'that I was doing my utmost to comply with the strategical requirements of N's plan, but in the matter of tactics I alone could decide'. The crux of the issue was whether (as Haig wished) to attack the Vimy Ridge, or advance further south (Nivelle's view): Lyautey, with all the authority of his personal prestige, came down on Haig's side. The con-versation showed signs of fading out; Nivelle, as Spears says, 'had not taken his cue'. Lloyd George was forced to intervene again.

The Prime Minister now stated that 'he did not understand about strategy and tactics. He would like it clearly stated what the respective responsibilities were.' This was a significant enlargement of the topic,

and it drew forth from Nivelle a general advocacy of
'Unity of Direction' for the whole period of the pro-
jected operations, including the preliminary and
'follow-up' phases. This was coming nearer to what
Lloyd George had in mind, but it was still not quite
there :

'He therefore asked the French to draw up their
proposals for a *System of Command* before dinner,
so that he, Robertson and I, could discuss it after
dinner. A subsequent Conference with the French
Government would then be held tomorrow morning
to finally decide.'[7]

Briand, an experienced conference-man, took the
opportunity of having inscribed in the minutes the
'perfect harmony' of all the delegates 'on the principle
of unity of command'. This brought the sittings of the
first day to an end, but not its drama. Robertson and
Haig did not much care for the way things were
shaping, but they still had no inkling of what was in
store. They chatted briefly before dinner, and at that
meal Haig sat among the French leaders. 'We had
quite a cheery talk.'

The French proposals were handed to Lloyd George
after dinner (from which he had absented himself on
grounds of 'illness') : he passed them straight to
Robertson, without comment. Haig, arriving in
Robertson's room shortly afterwards, 'found him most
excited'—a characteristic understatement of the
C.I.G.S.'s condition. Spears says : 'As a stimulus to
good digestion [the proposals] were a failure. Wully's
face went the colour of mahogany, his eyes became

perfectly round, his eyebrows slanted outwards like a forest of bayonets held at the charge—in fact he showed every sign of having a fit. "Get 'Aig," he bellowed to The Monument.'[8]

In truth, the typed paper which Robertson now held in his hands was an extraordinary document : what it set out, with precision and in detail, was a scheme for the complete integration of the British Forces in France into the French array, with a British 'Chief of Staff' at French G.H.Q. having direct access to the British Government, and reducing the role of the British C.-in-C. to that of a glorified Adjutant-General, dealing only with discipline and personnel.

'With none to warn them of the effect of their proposals on the British Army,' says Spears, 'the French had allowed a perfectly defensible idea to run away with them. Starting from false premises, but logically developed, the scheme had grown ever more precise in its fantastic assumptions, until the British Army, in the minds of those who worked it out, had ceased to exist as an entity. Its Commander-in-Chief had become a cipher, and its units were to be dispersed at the will of the French Command, like the Senegalese regiments, like the Moroccans, like the Foreign Legion, until its massed thousands had become mere khaki pawns scattered amongst the sky-blue pawns on the immense front controlled by the French from the North Sea to Switzerland.'

What we now know (but what was not then known to Haig and Robertson) is that the French document had been prepared beforehand at Nivelle's H.Q.

Hence, no doubt, some of his diffidence at the conference; but in fairness to Nivelle it must be admitted that he had reason to believe that in producing this paper he was simply doing what the British Government desired. The French, we may suppose, were somewhat taken aback at subsequent developments, which showed that Lloyd George had just been trying to use them in a personal intrigue against his chief military advisers. Even he, when he saw the French paper, and witnessed the reaction of the British soldiers to it, was somewhat shaken. Haig told him bluntly 'that in my opinion, it would be madness to place the British Forces under the French, and that I did not believe our troops would fight under French leadership. . . . He agreed that the French demands were excessive but insisted on R. and myself considering a "scheme for giving effect to the War Cabinet's decision".' With this cold comfort the soldiers retired, feeling that 'we would rather be tried by Court Martial than betray the Army by agreeing to its being placed under the French'. What disturbed them as much as anything was a hint from Hankey that ' "L.G. had not received full authority from the War Cabinet" for acting as he was doing'.

It was a bad night for Robertson and Maurice : on the one hand they faced this unspeakable French proposition, as dangerous as it was repellent; on the other hand, the damage of mass resignations and an open conflict between the Prime Minister and the Army leaders could be equally devastating. They received little support from Haig in their attempts to find a solution; no doubt conscious of how his personal implications might be interpreted, he contented himself with recording on paper the conviction that the proposed change in the command system was 'fraught with the gravest danger'. It was left to Robertson to explain this danger in detail to Lloyd George. It was a stormy and fruitless interview.

Corridors were now bustling with movement, as proposals and counter-proposals were devised, while British and French sought and made their mutual explanations. Nivelle professed himself astounded that Robertson had not known what was afoot; he blamed Bertier as an 'intriguer'. Lyautey assured both Haig and Robertson that he had known nothing of the French paper until he entered the train on the way to Calais. Both he and Nivelle spoke of the 'insult offered to [Haig] and the British Army'. Nivelle was dissembling—his Staff had drawn up the paper on February 21st—but there is no reason to suppose that the upright Lyautey was speaking anything but the truth. Between the two poles of Lloyd George's fixed intentions and Robertson's fundamental opposition to them, confusion grew. This was one of the most dangerous moments of the War, containing every possibility of an irretrievable clash between the British soldiers and politicians, and between the British and French Commands.

It was Hankey, whose role had so far been distinctly enigmatic, who finally discovered a formula of compromise. In essence, it amounted to this: Haig would be subordinated to Nivelle only *for a limited period* (the offensive in preparation); he would retain tactical control of the British Army; he would have a right of

appeal to the British Government in case of disagreement with Nivelle. With this the British soldiers had to
be content. Lloyd George asked Robertson whether, by
these terms, ' "Sir Douglas Haig was compelled to obey
Nivelle's orders like a French Commander", to which
Robertson answered that he was'. And with that, for
the time being, Lloyd George was content, too.

But satisfaction was short-lived. No sooner was the
agreement signed than Nivelle wrote to Haig in terms
which showed that, for him, the compromise was
merely a form of words : Haig was now a subordinate,
pure and simple. On March 3rd Robertson was la-
menting : 'We ought not to have *signed* the document
. . . I trusted to Nivelle to play the game. It all depends on him and I hardly dare trust him.' Nor did
the British War Cabinet greatly care for what had been
done in its name. By March 12th the unworkability of
the Calais proposals was so apparent that a second
conference had to be held in London; this time, with
all issues in the open, it was not difficult to reach a
saner position. It was now agreed that Nivelle should
communicate with the British Government only
through Haig; that the British Mission at French
G.H.Q. should be subordinate to Haig, not a source
of command to him; and that 'All the British troops
stationed in France remain in all circumstances under
the orders of their own chiefs and of the British Commander-in-Chief.' Haig appended his signature to
this, 'on the understanding that . . . the British Army
and its Commander-in-Chief will be regarded by
General Nivelle as allies and not as subordinates, ex-

cept during the particular operations which he explained at the Calais Conference'.

Yet it was not any formal convention, but the War itself that finally disposed of the Calais experiment. While the conference was still in progress, the Germans had begun their withdrawal to the Hindenburg Line which ended by depriving Nivelle of half of his proposed frontage of attack. In French military and civilian circles alike, doubts about him grew; when the Briand Government fell in March, the new War Minister, Painlevé, became the focus of these criticisms. By the time the great French offensive opened, Nivelle was already in semi-disgrace. But by now the British were already committed to their part in the enterprise, so that at last the truth became apparent, that what Lloyd George had achieved at Calais was not merely the subordination of the British Army to a foreign general, but its subordination to the Government which commanded that general. It lay within the power of the French Government to cancel the entire operation, as Painlevé was much tempted to do; in which case all the British effort and the lives lost would have been totally wasted. Instead, they were only largely wasted—through the breakdown of Nivelle's attack, which brought his prompt downfall. The only measure of clear success in the whole affair was that won by Haig's armies at Arras, including the storming of the Vimy Ridge, to which Nivelle had been opposed. But even this success was at the expense of the main British operation later in the year—'Passchendaele', which started at least six weeks too late to be successful.

So ended the first of Lloyd George's expedients to rid himself of his unwelcome military advisers, and avoid unpalatable political decisions. His supporters have tried to present this episode as an essay at that Unity of Command which came to pass in 1918, and was such a feature of the Second World War. But that view is impossible to sustain in the face of the evidence. The contrary truth was well expressed by Haig's Chief of Intelligence, Brigadier-General Charteris, as soon as he heard what had happened at Calais:

'The whole thing is exactly what many people warned us to look for in Lloyd George, but it has come sooner than any of us expected and with less reason. . . . I suppose the real reason at the back of it all is the hope that we shall win the war without many more British casualties. If that is so it is an amazing error of judgment. It is difficult to see why if the Cabinet wanted to have one supreme military authority, they did not press for somebody, either French or British, who would have been over both [Haig] and the commander of the French troops in France.'

This, as we know, was the solution finally adopted; but before that could happen, the Prime Minister's agile brain was still busy with devious devices.

PART II

In the warm sunshine of the belated spring of 1917, the British Prime Minister, Mr. Lloyd George, was a

man transformed. British successes and French failures
in the grim, wintry battles of April had had their effect.
Writing from Paris on April 21st to Sir Douglas Haig,
Lord Esher said : 'It is almost comic to see how the
balance has turned. For the moment, I do not think
you could do wrong.' On May 6th, he went further :
'[Lloyd George] has shelled off his Gallic proclivities
in a remarkable degree . . . his notions of French
superiority in everything are obliterated. He sees, with
his serene Celtic forgetfulness, the British Commander-
in-Chief and the British soldier, through a more
gracious stratum of air.' This was two days after a
significant Anglo-French conference in Paris; Esher's
comment confirmed Haig's own impression :

> 'Mr. Lloyd George made two excellent speeches
> in which he stated that he had no pretensions to be
> a strategist, that he left that to his military advisers,
> that I, as C.-in-C. of the British Forces in France
> had full power to attack where and when I thought
> best. He (Mr. L.G.) did not wish to know the plan,
> or where and when any attack would take place.
> Briefly, he wished the French Government to treat
> their Commanders on the same lines. His speeches
> were quite excellent.'

When the Prime minister visited Haig's headquarters
shortly afterwards, the same sentiment persisted : 'He
seemed quite converted in his views about the British
Army, was loud in its praises, and heartily congratulated me on the success of my operations.'

The rapprochement was short-lived. The opening
months of 1917 were filled with threatening events : in

March, a Provisional Government was formed in Petrograd, the Tsar abdicated, and the first stage of the Russian Revolution began; in April, the great French offensive that was to end the War in forty-eight hours failed dismally, bringing in its train the disgrace of the French Commander-in-Chief, General Nivelle, and a wave of disillusionment that spread dangerously through the nation and Army; at the same time, on the Italian front, successive attacks and counter-attacks piled up the mortality of the War, without clear advantage to either side; the entry of the United States into the conflict in April meant, for the time being, a further strain upon shipping resources already seriously menaced by submarine warfare, and a perilous temptation to war-weary nations to sit back and 'wait for America'.

The weight of all these happenings naturally affected Lloyd George, and to add to them he was conscious of serious symptoms on the British Home Front, expressing themselves most alarmingly in Labour disputes which cost the country 5,966,000 working days during the year; the worst period of all was April and May. Against this background, he viewed with increasing trepidation the plans of the British General Staff and General Headquarters for a major offensive in Flanders. Forgetting the Government's own initiative in demanding this offensive, and the Admiralty pressure behind it; ignoring inter-Allied agreements, Lloyd George saw in it now only the risk of another apparently futile 'Somme', with casualty lists which would yet further intensify the problem that he found most repugnant and insoluble—man-power.

Nevertheless, under the inexorable determinism of long-standing preparations,[9] in the absence of any feasible alternative that would not permit the enemy to recoup the losses he had sustained during the past year, and profit from the crumbling of Russia, and perhaps strike a deadly blow at France, during her period of dire weakness, the British offensive was launched. Starting terribly late, with most of the brief summer behind it, facing the worst weather and ground conditions of the War, poorly managed at first under the direction of the Fifth Army, and robbed of the French co-operation on which Haig had counted, but not without some striking achievements to its credit, the Flanders offensive finally foundered in the mud of Passchendaele. That was in November; but already, nearly two months earlier—and, oddly enough, at the very time that the British Army was about to make some progress—Lloyd George had sickened of the whole campaign, and with it the two generals whom he held responsible, Haig and Robertson.

So soon as September 5th, with the battle only five weeks old, and temporarily halted by drenching down-pours, Sir Henry Wilson noted in his diary:

'I believe that Lloyd George, knowing that Haig will not do any good, has allowed him to keep all his guns, etc., so that he can, later on, say, "Well, I gave you everything. I even allowed you to spoil the Italian offensive. And now, owing to gross miscalculation and incapacity you have entirely failed to do anything serious except lose a lot of men." And in this indictment he will include Robertson, and then get rid of both of them.'

Wilson had been out of employment for some months when he wrote this, and was not to know how wide of the mark was his idea of Lloyd George giving Haig 'everything'. The Army had entered the offensive with the infantry 99,000 below their establishment, while only three days before Wilson's diary entry Haig had been asked to part with 100 heavy guns from the French sector in Flanders to help the Italians, a request to which he reluctantly agreed on the following day.

Wilson's assessment of Lloyd George's main motive, however, was correct. He was thus not greatly surprised, a few weeks later, when the Prime Minister asked him and Field-Marshal Lord French (commanding Home Forces) to advise the Cabinet on strategic matters. 'In order to enlighten the Cabinet on the military position and to test and fortify my own judgment on the action which I was inclined to take, I decided to seek independent expert opinion', says Lloyd George. To Robertson, who as C.I.G.S. was the Government's official and *responsible* adviser, he explained this unusual step by saying that 'the patient after a three years' course of treatment not being yet cured, he thinks it advisable to call in another couple of specialists'. French and Wilson attended a War Cabinet meeting on October 11th; lacking information, they asked for a little time in which to prepare their views. Robertson agreed to supply them with 'all papers, etc., that we want'. Though irritated, he was not greatly disturbed; he told Haig:

> 'I do not much care what advice is rendered [by them] as I shall not budge an inch from my paper and I do not suppose you will budge from yours.'

French and Wilson submitted their views to the Cabinet on October 20th; their opinions about general strategy are no longer important, but what is important is the plea that both made for what French called 'a Superior Council of the Allies . . . to appreciate the general situation and formulate plans'. It is not open to doubt that, as in 1914, Lord French was deeply influenced by his voluble and persuasive junior. 'Superior Direction' was a theme-song which Wilson had been chanting for a long time. Three days before he completed his memorandum, he noted:

> 'It became very clear to me tonight that Lloyd George means to get Robertson out, and means to curb the powers of the C.-in-C. in the field. This is what I have been advising for $2\frac{1}{2}$ years, and this is what the whole of my paper is directed at—not to getting Robertson out, but to forming a Superior Direction over all the C.G.S.s and C.-in-C.s.'

Unconsciously, in this revealing entry, he displays the mixture of motives that lay behind what was always *both* a legitimate attempt at Unity of Command, *and* a deliberate manœuvre to hamstring the Government's responsible advisers.

What followed bore throughout the brand of this confused motivation. What Wilson advocated was 'the establishment of an intelligent, effective and powerful superior direction. And by this I mean a small War Cabinet of the Allies so well-informed, and above all, entrusted with such power that its opinion on all the larger issues of the War will carry the weight of conviction and be accepted by each of the Allies as final.' Lloyd George was much taken with this idea, and wrote shortly afterwards to the French Prime Minister, M. Painlevé :

> 'If we are to win the War, it will only be because the Allied nations are willing to subordinate everything else to the supreme purpose of bringing to bear upon the Central Empires in the most effective manner possible, the maximum pressure military, economic and political which the Allies can command. There is, I am sure, only one way in which this can be done, and that is by creating a joint council—a kind of Inter-Allied General Staff—to work out the plans and watch continuously the course of events, for the Allies as a whole.'

The Italian disaster at Caporetto (beginning on October 24th) produced a mood for far-reaching measures. A conference of Allied leaders was held at Rapallo on November 6th, at which Lloyd George and Painlevé, in complete accord, had no difficulty in obtaining acceptance of their ideas. A Supreme War Council was set up, and the fifth session of the Rapallo Conference became the first of the new body. This was to consist of representatives of the four governments, France, Italy, Britain and (later) the United States, assisted by 'Permanent Military Representatives', one from each Power, backed by Staffs, who would act as technical advisers without executive functions. The Supreme Council would meet at least once a month, and (after a wrangle with the French) its headquarters were to be at Versailles. Explaining its object to the House of Commons on November 14th, Lloyd George said that this was

'to set up a central body charged with the duty of continuously surveying the field of operations as a whole, and, by the light of information derived from all fronts and from all Governments and Staffs, of co-ordinating the plans prepared by the different General Staffs, and, if necessary, of making proposals of their own for the better conduct of the war'.

The sense of achievement in those who had brought about this result was as though they had won a victory over the enemy in the field. Others were less pleased. 'Sir William Robertson', says Lloyd George, 'ostentatiously declined to attend the discussions. . . . He left the room with a flaunting stride, the moment the idea of a Supreme Inter-Allied Council was mentioned. . . . He said : "I wash my hands of this business." ' To Wilson (present at Rapallo[10]) Robertson said : 'He does not see how it can work without responsibility, nor why it should be given responsibility. He thought that it might work if Maurice[11] was member, but not otherwise.' Robertson never departed from this view, which ultimately brought about his removal. Haig was less severe, but his objections were equally practical; remarking to Robertson that Ministers and governments were apt to change frequently in some Allied countries, he added :

'Judging by the past, our representatives are more likely to be permanent than are those of France and Italy, and we may gain a leading voice on the Council. I doubt much whether it will be a controlling voice however. In the past three years we have seen so much of the influence of the conflicting interests of States and of the failure of some Governments to realise that . . . the common good is the highest interest and should override all others, that I fear if agreement is reached at all on important questions of strategy it will be reached only by compromise— and the danger of action in war based on compromise is evident.'

With that said, Haig was prepared to agree that 'The object of ensuring common plans and co-ordination in executing them is of course admirable, and I think that as the Government has apparently decided on this Scheme all we can do is to try to work it until and unless we find that it is not possible to do so.' But his conclusion was : 'If it were still possible however to prevent this Supreme Council from coming into existence, I think it would be greatly to the interest of Great Britain to do so.' Haig's Chief of Intelligence Brigadier-General Charteris, was much sharper, and disagreeably prophetic :

'[The Supreme War Council] is utter rubbish so far as fighting is concerned. It will mean delay in any attack on the Germans and will break down at once if the Germans attack us. But it also means that the Cabinet is going to oust [Haig] or Robertson, or both.'

That this was, indeed, part of the object that Lloyd George had in view became apparent when the nominations of the Permanent Military Representatives came into question.

It was soon evident that the role of the British Military Representative would be significantly different from that of his foreign colleagues. As Haig had forecast, political instability in France became a factor: on November 13th Painlevé resigned after losing a vote of confidence, and on the 15th M. Clemenceau became Prime Minister and Minister of War. On the 27th, he announced that he wanted to make General Foch, the Chief of General Staff, French Representative at Versailles, and that he would like General Pétain, now Commander-in-Chief, to be represented there too. Wilson lamented:

> 'This would mean Robertson and Haig, and we should be where we have been all along. . . . Lloyd George is angry, and says that he will have a row with Clemenceau . . .'

Having a row with 'the Tiger' was rarely good business. The most that Lloyd George could procure was that, instead of Foch, General Weygand should represent France. This was a difference of name only, for Weygand was Foch's Chief Staff Officer and *alter ego;* he would be no more than a mouthpiece of the French General Staff. In the same way, the Italians appointed their ex-Commander-in-Chief, General Cadorna, who would also take a General Staff point of view. The Americans made no bones about the matter, and ap-

pointed General Bliss, their Chief of General Staff.
Lloyd George appointed Wilson.

As the latter's biographer says, Lloyd George's conception 'was that of a military expert who would be
wholly independent of his War Office . . . and would
be prepared to express views entirely different from
those entertained, as the case might be, by Foch or
Robertson, the officers who were responsible to their
respective Governments and to their respective countries. . . . Wilson's position was, in fact, going to be the
exceptional one . . .' Not only Wilson's position, but
Britain's; for the second time in 1917, at a moment
when her voice in the alliance should have been more
firmly asserted in accordance with her expanding
effort, Lloyd George's devices had ensured that it
would be uncertain and divided.

The unsatisfactory character of the new organ was
quickly seen. In the military field, it could investigate,
it could recommend, it could not act. As the consequences of the Bolshevik Revolution made themselves
felt, in particular the large accession to German
strength in the West, with the threat of a knock-out
blow at the Allies, action became essential. To Lloyd
George the Western Front was now anathema, and
he resolutely set his face against anything which might
stimulate more of the dreadful battles that had already
taken place there—forgetting that the enemy might
take a different view. The man-power problem which
he had so conspicuously failed to solve during his year
as Prime Minister now arose as a spectre. General
Smuts warned the War Cabinet (of which he was a
member) in January 1918 that the infantry of the

B.E.F. were 100,000 below strength. In the same month, contemplating the reinforcements that he was likely to receive, Haig expected to have to disband some 16-19 divisions. In the event, on the eve of the great German offensive, he was compelled to disband 141 battalions—the equivalent of nearly 12 divisions. To all protests, Lloyd George returned only two answers: he would, says Repington, 'threaten a Social Revolution if the country were asked for more men, and made the most of the argument'; or he would use his remarkable dialectical powers to score victories in discussion over his military leaders. The Germans were harder to beat.

It is interesting, indeed, grimly amusing, to observe the contribution of the Supreme War Council to the last great crisis of the War. Late in December, as evidence mounted of an impending German attack on the grand scale, Wilson and his Staff at Versailles mounted a 'war game', to fathom the details of German intentions. This was a procedure that always appealed to Wilson; and the section of the Staff that conducted 'enemy' manœuvres would turn their hats round back to front to heighten the illusion. Two conclusions were arrived at through these cerebral exercises: first, that no decision was likely on the Western Front during 1918, so that the Allies would do best to concentrate their efforts against Turkey; secondly, that the British should extend the front held by their attenuated army in France by forty miles, instead of the twenty-eight miles to which Haig had already sorrowfully agreed.

This 'war game' was repeated at intervals through

January for the benefit of awed visitors. When Lloyd George heard of it, he was 'much interested', says Wilson. 'He made several valuable suggestions, especially about the Boches not attacking in the west, but going for Odessa and the north of the Black Sea, and holding us off meanwhile.' Robertson, on the other hand, when he was told, was 'a good deal knocked about by all this'. Haig remarked that : 'The whole position would be laughable but for the seriousness of it.' He pointed out that such proposals raised 'the whole question as to the status of the "War Council" in an acute form. The Government now have two advisers ! Will they accept the advice of the Versailles gentlemen (who have no responsibility) or will they take my advice ?'

In the event, direct agreement between Haig and Pétain avoided the danger of further extensions of the British front; one shudders at what might have happened otherwise; what actually happened was bad enough. And it was agreement between Haig and Pétain which finally sealed the futility of the Supreme War Council as a war-directing agency. One of the few rational suggestions made by that body was for the setting up of an Allied General Reserve which would be interchangeable between the British, French and Italian fronts. In the straitened conditions of early 1918, the advantages of such a force were palpable. But the question was, where was it to come from ? An 'Executive Committee' was set up at Versailles, under Foch as chairman, to handle the Reserve, a decision, as Haig said, that 'to some extent . . . makes Foch a "Generalissimo".'

But he was a Generalissimo with no troops, for Haig

himself, in view of the weakness of his army and the increased length of his front, flatly refused to part with any men, and Pétain, who had insisted on the extension of the British front precisely in order to build up a reserve for his own armies, took the same view. The most that either would accept was that the British and French divisions in Italy—'the five divisions I sent there are really the Reserves of the British Forces in France,' said Haig—might be earmarked, or, failing that, an equivalent number of Italians, while the British and French remained in Italy. As to present emergencies, Haig and Pétain agreed to lend each other mutual support when the blow fell. And with that unsatisfactory arrangement, since the Supreme War Council was unable to persuade the British Government to revise its man-power policies, all had to be as contented as possible.

The weakness of the compact, of course, was that of all personal settlements—they depend on the personalities of the parties concerned. Wilson was being perspicacious when he wrote, on March 13th :

'Douglas Haig . . . said that, if I wanted a General Reserve, I must make some more divisions and I must get more man-power. I could not get him to see the problem in any other light. I impressed on him the fact that by refusing to contribute to the General Reserve he was killing that body, and he would have to live on Pétain's charity, and he would find that very cold charity.'

Wilson by now was no longer an adviser without responsibility; he was C.I.G.S. In that capacity, it fell to him, not only to deal with this fundamental question affecting the security of the Army, but also to administer the quietus to the Supreme War Council in the form that he and Lloyd George had originally conceived it.

The implications of the 'Executive Committee' had been too much for Robertson; he correctly saw in them a dangerous division of responsibility for the British Army's safety between Versailles and the War Office. This he could not accept, as a matter of principle. Even the offer of the Versailles post did not tempt him. 'An objectionable object in the middle of the table,' he said, 'is equally objectionable from whichever end of the table you look at it.' Robertson resigned, and Wilson went to the War Office in his place. Faced with this imminent prospect, he perceived in an instant the defects of his own brain-child :

'If . . . Robertson refuses Versailles, then Milner[12] and I agreed that he should put in someone junior to me, and let me have a directing voice at Versailles if I was C.I.G.S. The whole thing is rather muddlesome.'

Which was to say the least, for Wilson was making as a condition of his appointment the very stipulation that Robertson had made all along, and for which he was now being turned out. Lloyd George's ready acceptance of Wilson's proposition revealed his true motives in the whole affair.

So, by February 1918, a year's efforts by Lloyd George to rid himself of the two soldiers whose views he most detested had produced a victory. Robertson had gone, Haig remained. Unfortunately for the Prime Minister's theories, no sooner had Robertson departed, than his successor was forced to accept the same logic of events and the same conclusions which had made Robertson so unpopular with the Prime Minister. The main agent of these conclusions was, of course, the German High Command which, thanks to Allied failures in 1917, had now regained the initiative that it had seized in 1914, and only briefly lost.

The last expedient left to Mr. Lloyd George, which he now adopted, was the most desperate; it took the form of a flat refusal to face facts. Haunted by his revulsion at the Somme and 'Passchendaele'; fearing that Haig would, if permitted, renew these offensives; and fearing, too, the political implications of a sterner man-power policy, he attempted to justify the deliberate weakening of the B.E.F. by pretending that the danger of a German onslaught was unreal. On January 9th Haig recorded a 'cheery party' at 10 Downing Street :

'Derby bet the P.M. 100 cigars to 100 cigarettes that war would be over by next New Year. L.G. disagreed. I said I thought the war would be over because of the *internal* state of Germany. . . . The Prime Minister by cunning argument tried to get me to commit myself to an opinion that there would be "no German offensive," that the "German Army was done", but I refused to agree to his suggestion.'

On January 31st, after a meeting of the Supreme War Council, Haig recorded : 'Our shortage of men in the field had been demonstrated and Lloyd George had

shown himself anxious to prove by *figures* that we had
ample men on the Western front.' As late as March
14th, just a week before the Germans struck, the same
game was going on: 'I . . . had a long talk with the
P.M. and Mr. Bonar Law. . . . They did their best to
get me to say that the Germans would not attack.'

But the Germans did attack, and on the sector of
General Gough's Fifth Army, where fourteen diminished divisions were holding forty-two miles of front,
they scored an immediate and tremendous success.
Lloyd George, then and afterwards, was naturally at
pains to evade the responsibility for the disaster that
his policies had brought about. In April he told an
anxious House of Commons: 'Notwithstanding the
heavy casualties in 1917 the Army in France was considerably stronger on the 1st January, 1918, than on
1st January, 1917.' This statement was challenged in
a letter to the Press by General Sir Frederick Maurice,
who was still serving at the War Office until the end
of April. A critical debate followed in the House of
Commons, with a strong possibility of the Government
being overthrown. But Lloyd George was able to carry
all before him by the revelation that the figures on
which his statement was based had been supplied by
Maurice's own department. It was the end of the
Parliamentary revolt, and the end of Maurice's career
in the Army. 'Poor Maurice!' wrote Haig. 'How terrible to see the House of Commons so easily taken in
by a clap-trap speech by Lloyd George.'

For clap-trap it was. When Lord Beaverbrook's
book *Men and Power* appeared in 1956, it revealed a

portion of the diary of Countess Lloyd George for October 1934 :

'Have been reading up the events connected with the Maurice Debate . . . and am uneasy in my mind about an incident which occurred at the time and which is known only to J. T. Davies[13] and myself . . . I was in J. T. Davies's room a few days after [Lloyd George's] statement, and J.T. was sorting out red dispatch boxes to be returned to the Departments. As was his wont, he looked in them before locking them up and sending them out to the Messengers. Pulling out a W.O. box, he found in it, to his great astonishment, a paper from the D.M.O.[14] containing modifications and corrections of the first figures they had sent, and by some mischance this box had remained unopened. J.T. and I examined it in dismay, and then J.T. put it in the fire, remarking, "Only you and I, Frances, know of the existence of this paper." '

Lord Beaverbrook comments : 'There is no doubt that this is what Maurice had in mind when he accused L.G. of mis-statement.' What Maurice knew was the harsh reality of the 141 disbanded battalions, and the truth beneath the misleading statistics which showed :

Strength of B.E.F., January 8th, 1917 : 1,646,000.
Strength of B.E.F., January 5th, 1918 : 1,949,000.

What this concealed was the fact that 'Lines of Communication' personnel had increased by 399,450, while the numbers of 'fighting troops' had dropped by

78,500. No dialectical skill could alter this, nor the accompanying fact that, while from the opening of the year until March 21st (the date of the German attack) 174,379 reinforcements were sent to France, between March 21st and August 31st no less than 544,005 were sent *from the United Kingdom alone*. As the Official History says : 'It is obvious that the British Armies in France could have been brought up to full establishment before March 21st without unduly weakening the forces elsewhere had the Government so willed.'

The withholding of man-power was not quite the last of Lloyd George's expedients, but it was the last of consequence. Now it was Haig's turn, and in the crisis of the battle, when it became apparent that Pétain was prepared to accept a fatal division of the Allied armies, the French falling back to cover Paris, the British retiring on the Channel Ports, Haig asked and obtained the appointment of Foch as Allied Commander-in-Chief, over both Pétain and himself. This expedient worked inasmuch as Foch's resolute refusal to accept the possibility of defeat reanimated and cemented the cracking Allied line. But it was an expedient, nevertheless, though infinitely more disinterested than any that Lloyd George had produced. Because the War was won under a Supreme Commander, Lloyd George was always disposed to take credit to himself for urging the principle, and his followers interpret his various expedients as stages towards its fulfilment. Because, *in principle,* Unity of Command is unquestionably valuable, and because it became part of the apparatus of the Second World War military students have been inclined to over-write the significance of Foch's appointment. Sober reflection prompts one to doubt.

The ultimate truth about 1918 was accurately forecast by the British Intelligence Branch at G.H.Q. in January : 'If Germany attacks and fails she will be ruined.' This was the idea to which Haig clung throughout, though it sometimes spoilt his arguments with Lloyd George. But it was correct, and after the tribulations of spring the Allies were able, through failures in German strategy, to pass straight into their own victorious summer offensive.

Whether Foch could have survived otherwise may be doubted. Pétain, a sardonic but accurate observer, told Repington in September : 'Foch now has a position of great authority, though it largely depends on his being successful.' In a polyglot array such as the Alliance of 1918, this seems to be a correct assessment. Foch's system of command was a reversion to the obsolete personal leadership of earlier centuries; he had no Staff to speak of, certainly nothing remotely comparable to the large integrated Staffs that permitted Supreme Commanders to exercise leadership in the Second World War. That his system could have stood the stress of a long-drawn-out struggle is most unlikely. It is equally doubtful whether, with an alliance so composed, integration itself was practicable in 1918. In 1941-1945 this was much assisted by the fact that Britain and America speak (with minor variations) the same language; even so, we know that the strains were often considerable—as they were with the Germans and Austrians, enjoying a similar advantage, from 1914 to 1918.

In fact, Unity of Command, as Pétain percipiently remarked to Haig in 1917, is 'only possible amongst Allies when one Army is really the dominant one'. This was true of the French under Joffre; it was true of the Americans for the last part of the Second World War; it is true of N.A.T.O.; it was not true of anyone under Foch. His appointment was an ad hoc solution to an immediate crisis which prospered because circumstances turned in its favour. Lloyd George's attempt to take credit for this may be dismissed; invaluable as his role was in many ways, unique as was his contribution to winning the War, the fact remains that by some of his expedients he also came very near to losing it. Worse still, to the extent that his policies shaped the manner in which the First World War ended, they helped to make the Second inevitable.

NOTES

1. As Secretary of State for War.

2. It was widely, but wrongly, believed that U-boats based on these two ports were responsible for the larger proportion of sinkings.

3. Haig Diary, January 21st 1917.

4. Secretary to the War Cabinet.

5. Derby to Haig, March 3rd 1917.

6. Haig Diary.

7. Haig.

8. Major Lucas, Robertson's A.D.C.

9. Preparations for Messines, the first stage of the attack, began a year before.

10. Passing him on the battlefield of Marengo, Lloyd George told him : 'You are our Kellermann.'

11. Robertson's Deputy.
12. Now Secretary of State for War.
13. Lloyd George's Parliamentary Secretary.
14. Maurice.

1. "We are making a new world', by Paul Nash

2. Armistice celebrations in London, November 11, 1918
3. Ruins of Ypres, 1918

4. Lord Haldane

5. Admiral of the
Fleet Lord Fisher

6. General Nivelle

7. Lord Grey
of Falloden

8. Sir Douglas Haig at his desk, 1916

9. Allied leaders at 10 Downing Street: Foch, Clemenceau, Lloyd George, Orlando and Sonnino

10. Canadian pioneers at Passchendaele

11. Joffre

12. General Lanrezac

13. Field-Marshal Sir
William Robertson
and Marshal Foch
in 1919

14. French infantry during the retreat to the Marne

15. General Sir Henry Rawlinson

16. Lieutenant-General Sir John Monash

17. General Sir Herbert
Plumer and Sir
Herbert Lawrence,
Chief of General
Staff, with Haig

18. General von Bülow

19. Contrasts: *above* First World War landscape by John Nash
20. *below* Napoleon at Wagram, July 1809, by Carle Vernet

The mixture of dirt, danger and monotony which constituted the greater part of the trench warfare which lasted on the Western Front for four incredible years has taken on, in retrospect, the appearance of absolute martyrdom. This is not quite correct. Sidney Rogerson (whom I have already quoted) wrote: '. . . life in the trenches was not all ghastliness. It was a compound of many things; fright and boredom, humour, comradeship, tragedy, weariness, courage and despair.' Charles Edmonds explains this point of view a little further:

'Horror and discomfort, indescribable as they were, were not continuous. The unluckiest soldiers, whose leave was always stopped, who never had a "blighty" wound, spent but a small number of days in the face of the enemy, and of these only a few were of the most horrible kind. Their intensity, when they came, sharpened the senses and made the intervals correspondingly delightful. If no man now under thirty can guess the meaning of twenty-four hours' bombardment, nor has he any notion of the joy of ninety-six hours' rest. Who has never been drenched and frozen in Flanders mud, has never dreamed of the pleasure derivable from dry blankets on a stone floor.'

The contemplation of such blessings is salutary. It is largely hypocrisy to discover 'virtues' in war; yet it is hypocrisy too to pretend that there are none. The terribly simple satisfactions which enabled men to endure trench warfare indicate at least the virtues of constancy and resolution.

Fatigue and boredom were probably the worst erosions which the human spirit suffered in the trenches. 'Quite late in the war', says Edmonds, 'I have seen a man go to spend the afternoon in a trench under heavy shell-fire because he was bored with sitting in a safe dug-out.' From time to time this boredom was 're-lieved', or rather, abruptly shattered, by periods of the 'intensity' which he also mentioned. These, of course, were the great battles during which even the most alarming experiences of a front that was never altogether quiet at any time were exceeded beyond all supposition.

All through the War the Germans had to fight these battles on the Western Front for themselves; the intensity of their experience is thus beyond that of any of the Allies, and its effects were duly seen in 1918, when even the remarkable moral fabric of the German Army crumbled. Until 1916, the Allied cause was mainly upheld by the French, at a cost which brought about widespread mutinies in their Army the following year. In 1916 the British began to assume a chief role which they retained until the end of the War, and though it strained them to their uttermost they did not crack.

The style of battle changed profoundly during the four and a quarter years of the War. The three essays which follow may be regarded as a study of those changes : their contrasts could hardly be more marked. The first battle discussed was deeply significant, though it is scarcely known in Britain, because it was robbed of the participation of the British Army by an unfortunate decision, based as so often in war, on defective information.

THE BATTLE OF GUISE
AUGUST 1914

As soon as the main armies of France and Germany
met in 1914, the distinctive qualities of twentieth-
century warfare asserted themselves: the dominance
of the mechanical element—at that period expressed
through the use of the most highly developed railway
systems in the world, with the addition of motor transport, and the introduction of the aeroplane—and the
ascendancy of fire-power, which has reached its logical
conclusion in nuclear fission. In 1914, however, it took
the forms of massed artillery, with emphasis on the
heavy calibres, and the virtual substitution of the
automatic weapon, the machine-gun, for the infantryman's individual weapons, the rifle and bayonet.

The study of the craft of war, despite the ample
warnings given by the American Civil War fifty years
earlier, the Boer War, the Russo-Japanese War, had
not only failed to take into account the probable
effects of the astonishing material progress in every
industrial country, but had deliberately turned its
attention to the models of a too-distant past. Obsessed
by the superficial lessons of the Franco-Prussian War,
with its sensational results, both France and Germany
had permitted themselves to dwell upon mystical
factors as the secret of war itself: the search for an
infallible formula had taken the German General Staff

as far back as Hannibal's victory at Cannae in 216
B.C., and the French to the dangerous example of
Napoleon I. Paradoxically, this very stress upon mystical elements ended by giving to the First World War
that brutal, spirit-crushing quality by which it will
always be remembered.

For a few weeks, however, in August and early
September, the War retained some characteristics that
were intelligible to historians and Staff College students : it was a war of movement on open fields; there
was still some panoply; the first great crisis was intellectual, a crisis of generalship, not of matériel. Between
the opening actions and the Battle of the Marne, which
began on September 6th and reached its climax on
September 8th, the question was whether the vast
manœuvre known as the Schlieffen Plan could be
brought to fruition by the German General Staff
before the French Staff penetrated its meaning and
took the necessary steps to frustrate it. The Marne
decided that question. When the Schlieffen Plan col-
lapsed, Germany was left with no other large solution
to the impasse brought about by the assertion of material factors; France remained the prisoner of miscon-
ceptions which, by 1917, brought her Army to the
verge of ruin; and finally it was the British who, at the
price of immense suffering and bloodshed, hammered
out empirically a method of victory. But the Marne
was a triumph of generalship in the old style. And the
Battle of Guise, on August 29th, which, more than
any other single event, created the conditions for the
Marne, was a true old-style battle, one of the last to be
fought by European Armies.

By August 29th, the Battles of the Frontiers were over. The Schlieffen Plan appeared to have been successful at every point. The French, attempting to operate their own Plan XVII, had sustained a series of defeats without parallel in terms of loss of life and psychological impact. Their great offensive in Lorraine had been bloodily repulsed at the Battles of Morhange and Sarrebourg, and they had almost lost Nancy. Then, as the German threat to their left wing developed, still deluded by their false assessment of German strength and by their devotion to the spirit of the offensive, they had struck at what they believed to be the weak German centre in the Ardennes—only to sustain further shattering repulses at Virton and the Semoy. All their armies of the right and centre were in retreat by August 23rd. There remained the left wing, the Fifth Army, 250,000 strong, under General Lanrezac, and the British Expeditionary Force, 100,000

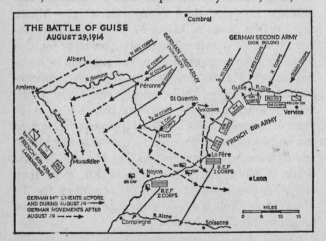

strong, under Field-Marshal Sir John French. It depended now upon this formidable mass of troops, who had only just come into contact with the enemy, to redress the balance.

The situation, as it appeared to the French Commander-in-Chief, General Joffre, and his Staff, on the eve of the Battle of Mons, on August 23rd, was that the Germans had shown themselves in great strength on the left, and in their centre; they could not be strong everywhere; it should be possible to roll up their right flank. On the other hand, there was growing evidence that their strength was increasing in that quarter; again, on the assumption that they could not be strong everywhere, they must be drawing troops from another part of the enormous battlefield, probably the centre. In that case, the Allied Armies of the Left must strike in a north-easterly direction to cut off the German right wing from the main body of their Army. In any event, the left wing must attack.

What the French General Staff failed to understand was the essence of the Schlieffen Plan, the deployment of enormous strength at the very outset. The Germans *were* strong everywhere, and nowhere stronger than on their right, where the great mass of manœuvre had been assembled that was designed to carry them round to the west of Paris, and end by pinning the French against their own frontier fortress system by an attack from the rear. Any advance by the Fifth Army and the B.E.F. could only thrust those forces into the jaws of the German array.

At this stage, human personality asserted itself, and events on the left flank of the Allied line, the crucial sector, where the Schlieffen Plan was expected to have its decisive effects, ceased progressively to be decided by Plan, and were decided more and more by the interplay of character among six men : Joffre, Lanrezac and French, on one side, and von Moltke, the German Chief of the General Staff, von Kluck, Commander of the *First Army,* and von Bülow, Commander of the *Second Army,* on the other. The first to be put to the test was Lanrezac. The enigma of General Lanrezac will probably never be solved; he is a figure of mystery; his period of high command in war was so short that we lack cross-references to judge him by. But during that short period, he seems to have been torn by one of those conflicts between intellect and character, the effects of which, certainly in war, are both searing and paralysing.

Lanrezac's reputation was made at the Ecole de Guerre, where, before the War, his lucid professorial analyses of exercises, the complete facility with which he was able to move pins and symbols on maps, or troops on manœuvres, had made a profound impression. It has been claimed for him that in regard to contemporary French theory—the doctrine of the offensive at all costs—he was always something of a heretic. He may well have been; but the fact remains that the Army that he was appointed to command was one designed to play a major part in the offensive prescribed by Plan XVII, and he was selected by Joffre for this command because he gave the impression of being ideally fitted for it. At the opening of the War, although the role of his Army was changed by the pressure of events, he was still regarded at the

Grand-Quartier-General as a fire-eater. Joffre, certainly, had no doubts about Lanrezac's offensive intentions in the early stages.

It is not, of course, particularly a criticism of General Lanrezac to say that his optimism and aggressiveness waned as he came closer to the enemy : were it not for the remarkable absence of such symptoms in the other French generals, one would consider that this reaction was merely normal. Only in the overheated condition of French military thinking at the beginning of the War were Lanrezac's doubts conspicuous; he himself probably felt this more acutely than anyone, and it is the most likely key to his subsequent odd behaviour. The role of his Army in Plan XVII was to form the left wing of the French offensive, beside the Third Army, with the Fourth Army held back as a Napoleonic Reserve. From the very opening of hostilities, however, Lanrezac began to feel his position on the extreme left to be disagreeably exposed. The able Intelligence Officers of his Deuxième Bureau began at once to collect ominous information, suggesting that there were far too many Germans in the vicinity of the Fifth Army for comfort, and that the enemy was developing serious threats to the French left. Already, by August 11th, Lanrezac was seeking and obtaining permission to move his leading Army Corps to Givet, near the Belgian frontier. The Fourth Army was moved up into line between the Fifth and Third Armies, and the following days saw a general taking ground to the left along the whole of this part of the French front. On August 15th Joffre agreed that the Fifth Army should complete its concentration in the area between Givet and Maubeuge, where the British Expeditionary Force would also assemble.

On the following day the Commander of the B.E.F., Sir John French, met Joffre, and on the 17th he met Lanrezac. These two meetings were of the utmost significance : their results were contradictory, and planted from the very outset that duality of feeling which endured in Anglo-French relations throughout the War. The meeting with Joffre was an unqualified success. The short, rotund, impulsive British leader took at once to the tall, massive, phlegmatic Frenchman; and Joffre, for his part, formed an impression of an ally who was entirely eager to help, and to come to grips with the enemy. The only drawback to this meeting lay in the fact that Joffre had just concluded, the day before, an interview with Lanrezac, at which that officer, despite his well-founded fears, had left his Commander-in-Chief convinced that he still believed unreservedly in the French Plan, and was itching to begin his attack. Joffre, therefore, spoke highly of Lanrezac to French.

But no sooner had Lanrezac returned to his own headquarters than he received more ominous news of German movements in front of him. He was still digesting this, and finding it a sour meal, when French visited him the next day. Lanrezac was one of many Frenchmen at that time—and we have not been short of similiar examples since then—who knew little of England, and disliked what they knew. Like many other French officers, he had small regard for the little British Regular Army. Pre-occupied with the grave problems of his own command, he was hasty, inconsiderate, and, indeed, downright rude to his British neighbour. Neither he nor Sir John spoke a word of each other's language, and yet they spent a short time closeted together without benefit of interpreter; the result was fatal. When Sir John, peering at a map, and stumbling over schoolboy French, asked Lanrezac whether he thought the Germans were attempting to cross the Meuse at a place with the impossible name of Huy, Lanrezac impatiently replied that they had probably merely gone there to fish.

The slight was obvious and unforgivable—the more so since it was this very German manœuvre which first exposed the dangers in store for the Fifth Army, and for the B.E.F. Sir John left the meeting with entirely un-neighbourly feelings towards Lanrezac, whose talents, he thought, had been much overrated; Lanrezac concluded that the British Commander was an ass, and wrote off his Army as another of those dubious formations, like Reserve divisions and Territorials, which could only be a hindrance to the serious work of war. But of one thing he left French, like Joffre, in no doubt—that he meant to attack the enemy. Yet, that very evening, in a message to Joffre, he mentioned the possibility of a retreat by the Fifth Army. This is the enigma of the man : his ideas, in the light of events, seem to have been well formed, more valid, indeed, than those of his superiors; but he lacked the character to stand up for them against the hostility which he knew they would meet, and even went so far as to conceal them from both his chief and his ally.

The following days saw the working out of this frame of mind on the field of battle. On the 20th,

Lanrezac was issuing orders for an attack to be prepared, but on the 21st he was speaking privately of
the folly of attacking, and it was, in fact, his own
Army that was attacked on that day. On the 22nd, he
was falling back from positions which he had described
as ideal for the defensive, and asking the B.E.F. to
help him by attacking his enemies in flank, although
he knew that the British were themselves threatened
by superior forces. On the 23rd, while they were
fighting the Battle of Mons in compliance with this
request, Lanrezac's Army was in full retreat. He even
forbade Franchet d'Esperey, the commander of his
1st Corps, to carry out a local counter-attack that
promised excellent results. On the 24th, when the
B.E.F. was disentangling itself with considerable difficulty and skill from its Mons position in the face of a
double encircling movement. Lanrezac rejected every
plea that he should assist the British, and continued his
retreat. He had undoubtedly been severely shaken by
his first experience of contact with the enemy, in which
his Army had fared no better than other French
armies all along the line; he had begun to doubt the
qualities of his own troops, and to talk of fighting the
war with artillery. His strategy was reduced to a
search for 'good artillery positions', where the famous
'75s could dominate the field. He became increasingly
vocal in his criticism of his own High Command.

The effect of this behaviour on Sir John French, a
choleric man at the best of times, scarcely needs to be
described. He conceived a powerful sense of having
been let down, of having exposed his Army—of having
risked, in fact, Britain's only Army—for the sake of an

ally who did not keep his word, who made no attempt to carry out agreed operations, who made insensate demands, and was, besides, personally unpleasant. Seriously threatened on his left, his lines of communication with his base and with the Channel endangered, he now found that he could depend upon no support on his right. The temperamental swing from the high optimism with which the British Staff had entered the War ('all over by Christmas') was violent; Sir John French was drawn into a gloom and despondency as unreal as his earlier hopes. On August 26th this feeling seemed to be confirmed by the most serious turn of events.

The day began with bad news from the right flank, where Haig reported heavy attacks on the British 1st Corps, separated from the rest of the Army by a gap of many miles. Shortly afterwards, General Smith-Dorrien announced that the 2nd Corps was incapable of further retreat and must stand its ground at Le Cateau. For a time it seemed to French that his whole Army would be lost. With this dreadful fear in mind, French attended his second, and last, meeting with Lanrezac, at British G.H.Q. at St. Quentin, with Joffre also present.

Joffre was deeply disturbed by the change in French, who seemed to him to have lost his balance. Belatedly aware now of where the real German threat lay, on his extreme left, he had already decided that he must meet it with new formations directly under his own control, in other words, a new French Army on the left of the B.E.F. His intention was to co-ordinate into this new plan the actions of French and Lanrezac.

But now he found that his ally, as well as being outside his command, was apparently incapable of further serious fighting. He was also developing grave doubts about Lanrezac, who seemed to have a rooted aversion to offensive action of any kind; and he discovered that the relations between these two key men had deteriorated to an extent which could only spell extreme peril to his whole left wing. It was essential to his purpose that they should delay the enemy as much as possible by local attacks and stubborn resistance, to give time for his new Army to assemble; yet both of them seemed to be sunk in the deepest gloom and to have no other idea than further retreat.

Joffre left the meeting very despondent; but it was not without its value, for from this moment onwards he became more and more clear in his mind that General Lanrezac was a liability which he could not afford. Ironically, none of the three generals perceived then, nor for some time afterwards, that the troops of the B.E.F. were, in fact, doing that day just what was needed of them, despite the gloom of their Commander. Haig's Corps had not been seriously attacked after all, and was now withdrawing in good order, while Smith-Dorrien was in the act of inflicting a sharp reverse on the enemy, before skilfully extracting his Corps from von Kluck's attempt to encircle it.

The next two days were crucial. And at this stage it will be well to turn to the German side, and consider what was going on there. For behind the façade of apparent universal victory, fatal hesitations and compromises were at work. The truth was that the Chief of the General Staff, Generaloberst Helmuth von Moltke, nephew of the great von Moltke of the Franco-Prussian War, was not the man to carry out a scheme so grandiose and venturesome as the Schlieffen Plan. Even before the War began, he had struck at the very fundamentals of the Plan by his redisposition of German forces, drastically reducing the proportion of superiority of his right wing to his left. He permitted himself to dream of a double encirclement of the French, of a victory in Lorraine as well as the great sweep through Belgium and Northern France.

On August 20th, Moltke's two left-wing Armies, the *Sixth* and *Seventh*, had attacked in Lorraine and inflicted sharp reverses on the French. They had been maintaining their pressure ever since. At the same time, the *First Army*, just beginning its swing to the south, had to detach two Army Corps to mask the Belgians in Antwerp. On the 25th, as bad news came in from the Eastern Front, Moltke detached two more Corps, again from his *right wing*, for the Russian front. And as the *First* and *Second Armies* swept past the fortress of Maubeuge, more troops had to be diverted for the investment of that place. It was thus a very reduced Schlieffen Plan which was being put into operation by August 27th. And to make matters worse, on that day, von Moltke freed von Kluck from the control of his senior neighbour, von Bülow, thereby weakening any chance of maintaining a cohesion which his own headquarters, far away in Coblenz, could never exercise.

The contrasting personalities of the two German commanders on the spot now came into play. Von

Bülow was a cautious, even timid, man, a firm believer in 'shoulder-to-shoulder' strategy, only happy when his flanks were secured by other formations. Despite his continuous success to date, his advances were slow and deliberate, and he seemed to fear traps everywhere. Von Kluck, however, sniffed victory in the air, even when it was a delusion. He was convinced that the British were routed and falling back towards the Channel Ports, and accordingly sent off his large cavalry force to the west to head them off. Astonishing though it seems, after the Battle of Le Cateau, which should have seen the destruction of Smith-Dorrien's 2nd Corps, not only did the Corps escape from the battlefield in broad daylight, but von Kluck then immediately lost it completely, swinging his whole Army south-westwards towards Amiens while the British retired southwards towards St. Quentin. Thus a gap arose between the two German Armies which made von Bülow very nervous indeed, while his flamboyant colleague went off in search of an illusory Cannae in the west.

Here at last was an opportunity of exactly the kind for which Joffre had been waiting—a chance to dislocate the enemy's encircling right wing while he built up his new Sixth Army on its outer flank. The first man to perceive the opportunity was Sir Douglas Haig, who, on the 28th, became aware of considerable German formations passing across his front, offering an excellent opening for a blow by his Corps and the Fifth Army. He immediately suggested such a stroke to General Lanrezac. At the same time Joffre visited that officer's headquarters, confirmed his misgivings about Lanrezac's frame of mind, and attempted to stiffen him by the issue of what is now known as a 'rocket', verbally, and by categorical instructions to counter-attack, which he set down on paper.

Joffre's idea was to strike towards St. Quentin, at the flank and rear of the *First Army,* not with any hope of crushing it, but to check it and delay its advance; this had now become all the more necessary because von Kluck was already in contact with the forward units of the Sixth Army. There was a danger that the Army might be devoured piecemeal as it assembled, which would have meant the end of all Joffre's hopes.

On the next day, August 29th, the whole complex of confusion and misunderstanding on both sides came to a head. It began with Sir John French. He and his whole headquarters were now sunk in a despondency which almost passes belief when one compares it with the attitude of the Corps Commanders who were in actual contact with the enemy. French had come to the remarkable conclusion that it was of imperative importance that his whole Army should be removed from the line of battle for at least nine or ten days, in order to refit. Drawing his inspiration from the prevalent mood at G.H.Q., the French liaison officer there reported to Joffre :

'Conditions are such that for the moment the British Army no longer exists.'

There was even talk among the Staff officers of transferring the British base to St. Nazaire, in Brittany.

Casualties, it was believed, had been ruinous; among other things, the entire Cavalry Division was thought to have been totally lost. Most of this was completely untrue, but, since it was believed, it is not hard to understand that Sir John French promptly forbade Haig to join in the offensive action which he had himself suggested, and rebuked him for having offered to do so. To Haig's disgust, he had to continue his retreat, and so the day began with the French being left alone. Yet now, at last, they were about to do the very thing that the British blamed them for not having done throughout the campaign.

At Lanrezac's headquarters there was intense activity. The task of the Fifth Army, even with British co-operation, would have been difficult enough. Without it, the thing became vastly more hazardous, but Joffre was determined that it should be done. He was, indeed, so determined, that he took the rare step of going personally to Lanrezac's H.Q. early that morning, and remaining there, saying little, making no attempt to run the battle, but watching Lanrezac's every move. If Lanrezac had faltered, Joffre would have removed him then and there. But, although he had one eye cocked distractingly over his shoulder at his Chief, Lanrezac did not falter.

He had, to begin with, to swing his whole Army round to face north-westwards, instead of north-north-east. On paper, with coloured pins, this is easy; on the ground, with tired, disorganised, in some cases demoralised, formations, it is anything but that. But by a prodigy of the staff work at which he excelled General Lanrezac pulled the bulk of his Army to face towards St. Quentin, and pushed his left and centre across the River Oise in the early hours of the morning. For a time they made slow though definite progress. Joffre was pleased to note the firmness and crispness of Lanrezac's handling of events, the spirit with which he checked any tendency to delay. And then the whole situation altered : as a French writer has said, 'there was a battle as willed by Joffre, and not by Lanrezac, but as Lanrezac and not Joffre had foreseen, it turned out to be far more a battle of Guise than a battle of St. Quentin'.

What happened was this : against the flank and rearguards of the German *First Army,* not in great strength, the French made progress towards the northwest. But shortly before noon their 3rd and 10th Corps, on the right of their advance, were checked by the arrival of new German formations from the north. These belonged to the *Second Army,* which was now well placed to take the French Fifth Army in flank. As the news of this untoward development came in, General Lanrezac displayed great nerve. He had in hand the whole of his large and relatively undamaged 1st Corps, under General Franchet d'Esperey. He was in the process of swinging this force across his line of battle from right to left, to make the final thrust towards St. Quentin. When news came in of serious reverses on the front of the 10th Corps, with pleas for help, Lanrezac replied :

'Le 10e Corps doit tenir coûte que coûte sur ses positions . . . Le 1er Corps doit continuer sa *marche vers l'Oise et n'intervenir du côté du 10ᵉ Corps qu'en cas d'absolue nécessité.'* ('The 10th Corps must hold its positions at all costs . . . The 1st Corps must continue its march to the Oise, and only intervene on the 10th Corps front in the case of absolute necessity.')

He issued an order to Franchet d'Esperey in this sense. But no sooner had the order gone than it became apparent that the 10th Corps, much tried in the earlier fighting of the campaign, would not hold. Lanrezac made up his mind instantly, and countermanded his order to d'Esperey, instructing him now to assist the 10th Corps in the direction of Guise. This swinging of units about on the battlefield was what pre-1914 generals had been trained to do; it was an exercise in the Napoleonic style which they understood; it was something that the conditions of the rest of the War would make impossible. But at Guise it worked.

General Franchet d'Esperey was a dynamic, aggressive and skilful officer. He was thirsting for a chance to attack the enemy, who had seen the backs of his troops too often for his liking. He threw himself into this attack, swinging his Army Corps in on both sides of the shattered 10th Corps, and facing it due north towards Guise, where the Germans were streaming across the River Oise. When he was satisfied that all was in order, he put himself, on horseback, with his Staff, at the head of one of his brigades, and gave the order to attack. As they went forward, d'Esperey called out to General Pétain, once a Staff College lecturer, and now commanding a brigade :

'Eh bien, Monsieur le Professeur à l'Ecole de Guerre, que pensez-vous de ce mouvement?'

Pétain's reply is not recorded : probably he made none, for he was a taciturn man. But the *'mouvement'* itself was all that could be asked for. The long lines of French infantry, in their dark-blue great-coats and red trousers, swept forward with fixed bayonets, drums and bugles playing, the colours unfurled at the heads of the regiments. A Napoleonic gesture, it was carried out in the Napoleonic manner, and for perhaps the last time in the War—in history—the manner was success-ful. The Germans were caught off balance, and thrown back into Guise. The cautious von Bülow fell back, and the Fifth Army saw the Germans in retreat for the first time. The Battle of St. Quentin had come to nothing, but the Battle of Guise was France's first offensive success.

It was not, of course, a success that could be fol-lowed up. The true Lanrezac reasserted himself the following day, with a surly refusal to withdraw unless he received categorical orders to do so. He had dis-sociated himself in advance from his victory, making it clear that he fought only under instruction; now he dissociated himself from the consequences. An error in the postal department of G.Q.G., which delayed his orders to retreat, almost brought about the destruction of his Army. He extracted it only in the nick of time. His whole performance, despite its tactical brilliance, had exposed the weakness of his character, and on September 3rd, the eve of the Battle of the Marne, Joffre replaced him by Franchet d'Esperey.

But Lanrezac's unwilling victory had done its work. For von Kluck, going full tilt towards Amiens and beyond, now swung his Army back in a ninety-degree turn to the south-east in response to von Bülow's appeals for help. This turn marked the final abandonment of the Schlieffen Plan. It gave the Sixth Army just the breathing-space it needed to become an effective force; it brought the Germans back into bewildering contact with the British, whom they thought they had destroyed, and made French's ideas of complete withdrawal impossible as well as ridiculous; finally, it brought the outer flank of the German right wing *inside* the net that Joffre had devised. The result was the Marne, one of the true decisive battles of history; but the Marne would have been impossible without the Battle of Guise. And the Battle of Guise owed everything to General Lanrezac, who had never believed in it at all.

The French Army lost over 200,000 men in the month of August 1914 alone. Fighting was continuous along the Western Front for the remainder of that year, as the battle-lines hardened out to the shape in which they finally petrified. While the Battle of Guise was being fought, other French Armies were resisting heavy attacks in Lorraine and Alsace. Then came the Marne, in which the Fifth Army, under Franchet d'Esperey, played a notable part, but in which the Fourth, Ninth and Sixth French Armies also participated strongly. After the Marne, the Aisne, and the first hint of deadlock; it was to break this deadlock by the old, well-tried manœuvre of turning a flank, that the so-called 'Race to the Sea' began. This drew the French into further battles along the Somme, in Artois and in Flanders, culminating in the First Battle of Ypres. The British have generally considered this to have been 'their' battle, because it was at Ypres that the Old Army met its end. Yet the truth is that all through 'First Ypres' the French were holding a longer front than the British, and their troops were far more numerous.

By the end of the year, it has been said, the French had lost about 800,000 casualties. Worse still, the Germans were firmly planted on French territory, as near to Paris at one point as Canterbury is to London. Their lines formed a huge bulge, the flanks of which were in Artois and Champagne. All through 1915, French strategy consisted in hammering at these flanks; two great Battles of Artois, and two Battles of Champagne, succeeded only in swelling the casualty lists by more hundreds of thousands. Then came Verdun, in 1916, with over 350,000 French losses, and after Verdun the Somme, where they lost 195,000, although the British by now were able to take the leading part.

Small wonder that by 1917 the French Army was exhausted, needing a long period of rest if it was to survive at all. Whatever was to be done on the Western Front during that year would evidently have to be done by the British. Yet one last *folie de grandeur* possessed the French High Command under General Nivelle; one last attempt was made to unlock the western barrier by the main weight of French arms. It failed; a great part of the Army mutinied; and for the rest of the year the British fought, to all intents and purposes, alone. The manner in which they did so, the weapons they used, the landscape they fought over, every attribute of their Flanders campaign, was a world removed from the conditions of Guise and the frontier battles of 1914. For this was 'Passchendaele'.

Passchendaele and Amiens

PART I—PASSCHENDAELE

Great changes in the art of war have frequently taken place in a very short space of time. Only four years separated the pedantic formalities of Valmy from Napoleon's rush into Italy; only five years separated the 'Peninsular' methods of the Crimea from the prototype of modern warfare waged between the American states; one week in South Africa transformed the outlook of the British Army; a year and a week divided the battles of Passchendaele and Amiens, the former a symbol of the waste and suffering of the First World War, the latter a prophetic glimpse of the mechanised manœuvre of the Second.

The word 'Passchendaele' has evoked more horror and loathing than any other battle-name in our history. Those who were there have never felt that they could entirely express what they saw and endured : 'nothing that has been written is more than the pale image of the abominations of those battlefields . . . no pen or brush has yet achieved the picture of that Armageddon', wrote a war correspondent of the day. Its influence, through those who were associated with it, extends into our own time. The morbid significance of Passchendaele is largely due to the late Earl Lloyd George and a group of military writers in the 'twenties and 'thirties who shared and amplified his views. The result has been a distortion of history and a deep injustice, both to the troops who fought this bitter campaign and to the generals who directed it.

Lloyd George has described Passchendaele as 'one of the most gigantic, tenacious, grim, futile, and bloody fights ever waged in the history of war'. He has frankly indicted the 'vanity' and the 'stubborn and narrow egotism, unsurpassed amongst the records of disaster wrought by human complacency', of the Commander-in-Chief, Sir Douglas Haig, and the C.I.G.S., Sir William Robertson, who directed the battle. In this he has been supported by such soldier-writers as the late Brigadier-General Baker-Carr, a machine-gun expert and tank commander of unorthodox outlook, who wrote : 'The Third Battle of Ypres . . . will ever remain an example of British stubbornness and British stupidity'; by General J. F. C. Fuller, who has told how Tank Corps H.Q. was instructed by G.H.Q. to discontinue sending in its daily 'swamp-maps', whose discouraging information belied the optimism of the Staff; by Captain B. H. Liddell Hart, who has written : '. . . there is little doubt that Haig's real motive was a strange belief that he could defeat the German Army single-handed in Flanders'; by Brigadier Desmond Young, who cried out in *The Spectator* in 1957 : '. . . let no one seek to justify or excuse the Battle of Passchendaele'; and by many others, among whom may be included Sir Winston Churchill, Mr. Edmund Blunden, and Siegfried Sassoon, with his memorable lines :

'I died in Hell—
(They called it Passchendaele). . . .'

The Official History of the battle did not appear
until 1948, by which time men had much else to remember and argue about. Even so, it caused a certain
stir. The cool tone and expository manner of the text,
coupled with a strong and conclusive preface, dealt
severely with the critics of the General Staff. This produced an angry response from at least one of them.
Captain Liddell Hart, who once dedicated a book to
the late Brigadier-General Sir J. E. Edmonds (the
Official Historian) in these terms : 'To "Archimedes",
who knows more of the history of the War than he will
ever write, but to whose guidance all others who would
write of it will ever be indebted', was publicly referring
in 1957 to the 'preposterous assertations of General
Edmonds' and to 'the way he "cooked" the figures.
. . .' But the Official Historian's view does not lack
support. The Australian Archivist has some striking
passages about the later stages of the fighting. Haig's
diaries (published in 1952), although insufficiently explicit, for the first time exposed an authentic three-
dimensional view of one of the most reticent and un-
fathomable generals in our history. German opinions
and accounts have mainly tended to confirm the cor-
rectness of our official version. And leaving aside
frankly polemical works, evidence has mounted up
which illuminates the motives and methods underlying the event, and makes some kind of objective
statement possible at last.

Some battles are easy to understand : some are not.

Waterloo, for example, or Alamein, are easy; Napoleon was fighting for an empire, Rommel was fighting for Egypt. Both had to be stopped and smashed. There were almost no complications. On the other hand,

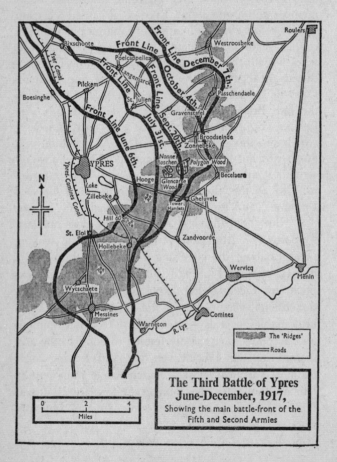

The Third Battle of Ypres
June-December, 1917,
Showing the main battle-front of the
Fifth and Second Armies

nearly everything to do with the Crimean War, or the Italian Campaign in 1943, requires explanation, frequently complex. Passchendaele was a similar case. It will help to discard the very name, with its emotional associations, and to call the battle by its official title, the Third Battle of Ypres. Within that title, two subsidiary battles can correctly be called 'Passchendaele'. What were the origins of 'Third Ypres'?

The advantages of using the right name are immediately apparent; it is not possible to view this great campaign of 1917 except in relation to the whole strategy which brought the British Army to the Ypres Salient in 1914 and embattled it there for the rest of the War. The Flanders front, apart from its allure as a traditional British battleground and its political significance as the last free strip of Belgian soil, embodied two ideas, one defensive—the protection of the Channel ports; one offensive—aiming first at turning, later at breaking, the extended German right flank, cramped in the narrow area of western Flanders. These concepts were the strategic realities : the tactical reality was the Salient. Shaped by the hazards of the First Battle of Ypres in 1914, dented by the gas onslaught of 1915, bulged first this way and then that throughout 1916, the Ypres Salient was at once a symbol of the heroic stubbornness of the British soldier and a thundering nuisance to his generals. Overlooked on three sides, with its only communications through the bottleneck of the shattered town, it became a dreadful liability. The idea of breaking out of the Salient steadily assumed a major significance in its own right.

Two events in 1916 helped to draw the British High
Command inexorably towards a major operation in
this area. The first was the Battle of the Somme. This
engagement, which was in truth by far the most terrible experience that the British Army has ever passed
through, was dictated by the exigencies of the French
Alliance—by the German attack at Verdun and by
Joffre's conviction that unless the British actually
fought beside him they would not pull their weight. It
was originally planned as a French battle with British
support, but as the French Army passed through the
remorseless mincing-machine of Verdun, the British
share in the Somme became preponderant. As a battleground the area had nothing to commend it. The
German positions, at the very nose of their huge
salient, were immensely strong. There was no possibility of surprise. There was no valuable strategic prize
ever in view. Four and a half months of bitter fighting
won no more than a narrow wedge of mud at an enormous cost in British lives. Haig, who had never had
much confidence in the French and distrusted too close
collaboration with them, was reinforced in his determination to make his next large effort as far away as
possible from his Allies.[1]

Then, towards the end of 1916, the Admiralty
became seriously worried, one might almost say panic-
stricken, about the menace of German submarines
operating from Ostend and Zeebrugge. Allied shipping
losses were averaging 300,000 tons a month, and this
was before the declaration of unrestricted submarine
warfare. On November 21st, following a meeting of
the War Committee on the previous day, Mr. Asquith

handed an unsigned paper to the C.I.G.S., General
Robertson, which contained this sentence: 'There is
no operation of war to which the War Committee
would attach greater importance than the successful
occupation, or at least the deprivation to the enemy,
of Ostend, and especially Zeebrugge.' This paper was
never signed, and therefore never had the force of an
official instruction. But there can be no doubt that it
played a significant part in reinforcing the British High
Command's intention to make its next attack in
Flanders.

Thus, before the end of 1916, there existed a powerful array of motives for this decision. To sum them up,
in a rough inverse order of priority, they were: to
secure the Channel Ports once and for all; to break
out of the Salient; to eliminate the German submarine
bases in Belgium; to strike a heavy blow at the German Army on its extended right flank. There was also
the secret wish to keep away from the French, although
it was never intended to fight alone. It was agreed with
Joffre that the French would simultaneously conduct
a large-scale offensive, so that the enemy should not
be able to mass reserves against either one of the
Allies.[2] The events of 1917 brought disappointment on
almost every count, but only the most jaundiced view
could regard these motives as insensate.

Two profoundly significant changes took place at
the turn of the year, one in Britain, one in France. Mr.
Lloyd George replaced Mr. Asquith as Prime Minister,
and General Nivelle replaced General Joffre as Commander of the French Army. From the moment of Mr.

Lloyd George's accession, confidence between the British Government and its military leaders was exposed to the severest strain, matched, from the moment of Joffre's departure, by the decline of confidence between the Allied High Commands. Both developments augured ill for the great but difficult operations that were being planned. The stress of war was itself intensified by the stepping-up of the German submarine warfare to a pitch that cost the Allies over 2,000,000 tons of shipping in the three months of April, May and June, and by the outbreak of revolution in Russia in March, from which time no aid could be counted on in the East. America's entry into the War in April was a comfort very much for the future. It was, in fact, over a year before American troops intervened in the fighting in any strength.

As 1917 opened, however, it was General Nivelle who represented the greatest hazard. His promotion to the chief command was symptomatic of the decline of French national morale. He had been responsible for two brilliantly conducted small-scale counter-offensives at Verdun, whose complete success and small cost contrasted most favourably with Joffre's massive and expensive failures in Artois and Champagne and on the Somme. He was promoted over many talented seniors —Castelnau, Foch, Pétain, Franchet d'Esperey and others—on the strength of his positive assurance that he could repeat these successes on the great scale. France was becoming desperate; Nivelle promised her a remedy, also desperate, but apparently sure. His plan had the simplicity of genius—or lunacy. He argued that his little victories at Verdun had proved that the enemy's front could be broken at any time; the problem was to exploit the rupture. This, he claimed, could be done by extreme violence and huge mass—'one and a half million Frenchmen cannot fail'. If a great victory was not won in forty-eight hours, said Nivelle, he would break the whole thing off. There would be no more Sommes.

The extraordinary thing is that he succeeded in making people believe in this wild adventure. In fact what he was saying was only what Joffre, Foch, and a dozen other Allied generals had preached and failed to accomplish for years; there was nothing new in it at all. On the contrary, as regards the development of the art of war, Nivelle's plan was reactionary, a throwback to the doctrine of the offensive *à l'outrance* of 1914. But he possessed what other soldiers lacked, a pleasing personality and a plausible discourse. He was certainly not afraid to talk; after the oracular silences and cryptic communiqués of Joffre and Haig, the liquid, ample, tempting utterances of Nivelle were a tonic and a joy. He not only persuaded his own Government; he also won over Mr. Lloyd George. In spite of all the latter's scepticism on the subject of offensives on the Western Front, Lloyd George believed wholeheartedly in this, the worst-founded of them all. And not without his reasons, for Nivelle could speak English as fluently as he spoke French, so Mr. Lloyd George had no difficulty in understanding him; and as a phrenologist, the British Prime Minister was able to see at once that the bumps on Nivelle's head were deserving of every confidence. He was so carried away that he forthwith took the remarkable decision to place the British Commander-in-Chief, Haig, actually under Nivelle's orders.

The Calais Conference, in February 1917, provided the occasion for attempting to carry out this scheme. Lloyd George confided in no one, and not unnaturally he provoked a violent reaction in both Haig and Robertson when they discovered what he was about. With the skilful aid of Colonel Hankey, then Secretary to the War Committee, the two incensed generals managed to procure a modification of the French proposals for a complete subordination of the British Commander-in-Chief which Lloyd George was eager to accept. The degree of subordination was carefully defined, and its duration limited to the course of Nivelle's great operation. Such was his self-confidence that all he asked of Haig, by way of support in this, was a preliminary diversion at Arras. As regards the British attack in Flanders, the preparations for which were already begun, his view was that it would never materialise because his own success would make it unnecessary.

Unfortunately the enemy was not disposed to fall in with Nivelle's plans. Nivelle made no attempt to keep these secret since he could see no possible obstacle to their complete fulfilment. Like almost every other French general (and, regrettably, like most of ours, too) he never permitted the thought of strategic withdrawal to cross his mind. Nor did he take any account of the tactical withdrawal which is the basis of the idea of defence in depth. Consequently the German retirement to the Hindenburg Line in March on a wide

front took him entirely by surprise and immediately
dislocated the whole northern sector of his attack. Per-
severing nevertheless in dreadful weather, and in the
face of the growing doubts of his senior generals and
political chiefs, the following month he thrust the
French Army into the carefully prepared German defensive zone behind the Chemin des Dames, where it
lost 115,000 men in ten days and utterly failed in its
stated purpose. The effects of this failure were stupen-
dous; they are still being felt in France today. They
were to sound like a knell through the rest of 1917.

The British attack at Arras, mainly conducted by
General Allenby, was conceived as a limited operation,
whose main purpose was to divert German reserves
from the French front, and whose secondary object
was to capture Vimy Ridge.[3] Both were achieved, by
careful planning and ingenious method. Within its
original framework Arras was a considerable success;
but the complete failure of the French created a new
set of conditions, and now Haig had to continue with
this operation far beyond the time intended. In fact, it
extended from April 9th until May 23rd, using up
troops and munitions which should have been available
for Flanders, and above all using up time. The heavy
casualties at Arras were bad enough; the lost summer
weeks were disastrous. But one thought emerged from
this misfortune which comforted British G.H.Q. Allenby's initial success confirmed the belief that the
enemy's line could be broken; it remained to be seen
whether the British Army could make a better job of
exploitation than the French. It was certainly in better
shape; Mr. Lloyd George was entirely correct in

saying: 'The British Army was the one allied army in the field which could be absolutely relied on for any enterprise.'

And now the time had come to start upon the enterprise. From the beginning of June until midway through November all attention was to turn on Ypres. There were plenty of misgivings; Mr. Lloyd George (soured by his disappointment in Nivelle) and many of his Cabinet colleagues hesitated and vacillated. On May 4th, in Paris, presumably in a mood for making amends, he gave Haig a free hand in the matter of further operations: '. . . I, as C.-in-C. of the British forces in France, had full power to attack where and when I thought best. He did not wish to know the plan, or where or when any attack would take place. . . . His speeches were quite excellent.' Accordingly, the following day, Haig jotted down his immediate intentions: (i) local wearing-out attacks on the Arras front; (ii) an attack on the Messines-Wytschaete Ridge in early June, having as its object 'the capture of the high ground and observation, thus securing the right flank and preparing the way for the undertaking of larger operations at a subsequent date directed towards the clearance of the Belgian coast'.

'At a subsequent date . . .'; therein lies the rub. General Plumer's attack at Messines on June 7th was one of the completest victories of the war. The main feature of it was the explosion of nineteen huge mines along the enemy's position, followed by a tremendous and accurate barrage. As a result our troops were immediately successful all along their line, and their casualties amounted to no more than one-fifth of

those anticipated.[4] The whole south-eastern face of the
Ypres Salient was cleared at last; a flying start, one
might have thought, for the great battle. But instead, it
was from this moment that the disappointments and
mischances of 'Third Ypres' date. The very success of
Messines seems to have had an ill effect, for once again
meticulous preparation had achieved a break-through
which seemed to hold the promise of sensational results if properly pushed home. Plumer's instructions
were to fight a limited battle, and, indeed, his tempera-
ment inclined him at all times to caution and delibera-
tion. There was a widespread, if unjust, feeling that a
great opportunity had been lost. The 'thrusting' Army
Commander of the B.E.F. of 1917 was Gough, and it
was to his Fifth Army that Haig transferred the main
role in the next phase of operations. The first task given
it was to take the Passchendaele-Staden Ridge and to
clear the low country between the Ridge and Dixmude.
Then, in conjunction with an amphibious attack by
Rawlinson's Fourth Army at Nieuport, the Fifth Army
was to advance towards Bruges and Zeebrugge. The
Second Army, under Plumer, was simply to 'cover and
co-operate with the right flank of the Fifth Army'. In
Haig's instructions to his Army Commanders this
sentence appeared : 'In the operations subsequent to
the capture of the Passchendaele-Staden Ridge opportunities for the employment of cavalry in masses are
likely to occur.'

Two major errors can be detected in this plan. First,
there was the transfer of the main role from Plumer,
who had commanded in the Salient continuously from
1915 and who had carried out all the preliminary

planning for this campaign, to Gough, who had to familiarise himself with the situation and reshape the plan for the expected quicker penetration and exploitation. This cost more valuable time, while the wet season in Flanders drew inexorably nearer. Secondly, there was the maleficent influence of the Admiralty's preoccupations with Ostend and Zeebrugge. This had the effect of pulling the Army off its true axis of advance, the central slopes neighbouring the Messines-Wytschaete Ridge, into the level, watery plain behind the coast. The Passchendaele-Staden Ridge was a correct objective, but the chances of seizing it were immensely diminished by prolonging the attack westward to Dixmude while the Second Army, on the right, remained passive. Inspired, no doubt, by the successful openings of Arras and Messines, there was a false confidence at G.H.Q., reflected in the reference to cavalry; one can easily see how unwelcome General Fuller's ominous swamp-maps must have been. But as Plumer had planned it, and later fought it, the battle could have been won.

These defects were internal, arising out of the British plan itself. There were other, even graver, problems stemming from the political direction and the French alliance. The latter had reached a most critical phase, of which Haig only became fully aware on June 2nd, and the British Government much later, if, indeed, at all. In all his planning Haig had counted on a French supporting attack; after Nivelle's disaster he realised that this was likely to be small, but Nivelle's successor, Pétain, had certainly not indicated that it would completely fail to materialise.[5] Then, on June 2nd, five

days before Messines: 'The Major-General of the
French Army arrived about 6.30 p.m. and stayed to
dinner. His name is General Debeney. He brought a
letter from General Pétain saying that he had com-
missioned him to put the whole situation of the French
Army before me and conceal nothing. The French
Army is in a bad state of discipline. . . . This would
prevent Pétain carrying out his promise to attack on
June 10th.' What had happened was nothing less than
a full-scale mutiny; only two French divisions had remained steadfast. The period of complete anarchy was
over by June, but neither Pétain nor Haig could have
had any further illusions about France's role for the
rest of the year.[6] This unforeseen complication now
became a dominant factor which influenced the whole
operation thereafter.

The French General Staff was particularly anxious,
for obvious reasons, to conceal the extent of the Army's
collapse. A few French political leaders had to know,
and there was no concealing events from civilians in
the zone of operations. As a matter of honour, as well
as of expediency, Haig had to be told; but the information was imparted in the strictest secrecy. He did not
feel entitled to take the British Government into his
confidence; the Government, meanwhile, was losing
confidence in him. Mr. Lloyd George had undergone
a change of heart since his magnanimous gesture in
May; on June 8th, the day after the Messines attack,
he set up a Cabinet Committee to reconsider the forthcoming Flanders offensive. The Committee did not
meet until June 19th when Mr. Lloyd George voiced

all his misgivings; his main concern was about casualties, a feeling with which one can easily sympathise (though it is hard to escape the truth of Sir Henry Wilson's tart remark to Mr. Bonar Law on July 7th: 'The loss of men might have been a good reason for not entering into a war, but a bad reason for not fighting when in the war'). Sir Douglas Haig, in an outwardly ebullient mood, explained his plans: '. . . he spread on a table or desk a large map and made a dramatic use of both his hands to demonstrate how he proposed to sweep up the enemy, first the right hand brushing along the surface irresistibly, and then came the left, his outer finger ultimately touching the German frontier with the nail across. . . .' Mr. Lloyd George never forgave that fingernail.

But on the following day the Committee was presented with something even more startling than a field-marshal's hands moving over a map. Admiral Jellicoe, the First Sea Lord, on being consulted about the need to clear the Belgian coast, 'stated categorically that unless that were done the position would become impossible and . . . we could not go on with the war next year through lack of shipping. . . .' Haig, as amazed as anyone, remarked: 'This was a bombshell for the Cabinet and all present.' Jellicoe, however, was quite positive.

Neither the optimism of his Army commander nor the pessimism of his chief naval adviser convinced the Prime Minister. But in the face of their testimonies an impasse was reached, reflected in the division of the Committee. General Smuts and Mr. Balfour, with Lord Curzon to a lesser degree, were in favour of going ahead with the offensive. Mr. Lloyd George, Mr. Bonar Law and Lord Milner were against. There was no casting vote. And so, says Mr. Lloyd George, 'it was therefore decided that I should once more sum up the misgivings which most of us felt and leave the responsibility for the decision to Sir William Robertson and Sir Douglas Haig. . . .' The post-Second World War student may call this admission pathetic, but can find another word for the recriminations that followed.

June was moving to its end and there were further contortions of the political animal are as astounding as of his Army, Pétain felt compelled to adhere to what had become a settled policy of the French Government, that the British left flank should under no circumstances be permitted to rest on the sea. There was a fear in France that otherwise the British would never leave the Pas-de-Calais: the only comment that it seems necessary to make on this is that the spiritual contortions of the political animal are as astounding as they are limitless. For Haig it meant more confusion and delay while General Anthoine's First French Army was inserted on the left flank of our Fifth Army. The help this French Army could bring did not outweigh the disadvantage of waiting for it to deploy. Sir Henry Wilson, who had earlier confided to his diary the sarcastic comments of Pétain and Foch on Haig's plans, told him on June 28th: '. . . that I did not think the French would be able to make another serious attack this year . . . and that, as one of our main objects now was to keep the French in the field, I was absolutely convinced that we should attack all we could, right up to the time of the mud. . . .' Pétain confirmed Wilson's view with a letter to Haig on June 30th in which he said: '. . . *l'offensive des Flandres doit être assurée d'un succès absolu, impérieusement exigé par les facteurs moraux du moment.*' ('. . . The Flanders offensive should be assured of a complete success, which is absolutely required by present considerations of morale.')

There was still a month to go before the offensive could open at last, on July 31st, fifty-four days after Messines. The enemy, of course, was fully alerted; the summer was well advanced and about to play a scurvy trick with an August rainfall that was double the average, and 'over fives times the amount for the same period in 1915 and 1916', according to the Commandant of the Meteorological Section at G.H.Q.

When the battle began, the first of the nine separate actions listed under 'Third Ypres' in the Official History—the Battle of Pilckem Ridge—set the tone of much that was to follow. In three days it carried the line forward to a maximum depth of 3,000 yards at a cost of 31,000 casualties; several thousand prisoners were taken, a lot of German dead were counted, some guns were captured. Compared with the 57,000 casualties for almost no result at all on the first day of the Somme, this was a success. Compared with Messines, or Vimy, and in relation to the objectives set, it was a failure, but not a sufficiently sensational one to compel a change of plan. In consequence the Fifth Army continued to attack in drenching rain across ground which the Official History describes well enough: '. . . the shelled areas near the front became a barrier of swamp, four thousand yards wide. . . . The margins of the overflowing streams were transformed into long stretches of bog, passable only by a few well-defined tracks which became targets for the enemy's artillery; and to leave the tracks was to risk death by drowning.' In this nightmare landscape, under the most trying and discouraging conditions, the Fifth Army staggered on to the two complete failures known as Gheluvelt Plateau and Langemarck.

By the end of August it was evident that things had gone seriously awry. Over 3,000 officers and 64,000 other ranks had fallen; 'discontent was general'. Haig decided to switch his main effort from the low ground to the ridges on the north-eastern face of the Salient, where it should have been all along.

From now on the main fighting passed under the control of General Plumer, whose Second Army became the spearhead. Nothing more was heard of the amphibious landings. The whole tactical concept was revised. Plumer's method was the carefully prepared, limited advance, step-by-step, approximately 1,500 yards at a time, of which 1,000 yards would be saturated by the initial barrage. He was a firm believer in guns. He asked for three weeks to prepare his first attack, and for over 1,300 guns and howitzers to carry it out. These, with 240 machine-guns, laid down five belts of fire along the whole front of attack, a density of one piece of artillery to every 5.2 yards. When Plumer's first attack came, it was a model of fore-thought and precision. At the Battle of the Menin Road Ridge on September 20th, four divisions, two Australian and two British, attacked on a 4,000-yard frontage with double the weight used on July 31st. The barrage, wrote General Birdwood, commanding the 1st Anzac Corps, 'was magnificent—quite the best the Australians had ever seen . . . the infantry, followed behind and occupied all the important points with the minimum of resistance. . . .' When the early mist rolled away, records the Official History, 'the sight that met the eye brought the thrill of victory always hoped for but so seldom experienced in previous offensives'. All the objectives were taken, except on the extreme right, and all counter-attacks beaten off.

This was the first of three operations at deliberate intervals which run in every respect counter to the Passchendaele legend. Each one of them was an unmistakable victory; and all three were fought under favourable weather conditions. Indeed, the Battle of Polygon Wood on September 26th was somewhat hampered by the fact that 'the ground was now so powdery and dry that the bursts of the high explosive shell raised a dense wall of dust and smoke. . . .' At Broodseinde, shells were observed to ricochet off the hard ground. In each of these three victories under General Plumer the Australian and New Zealand divisions played a notable part. Their great day was Broodseinde on October 4th, which the Germans have called 'the black day', and on which the Australian official account records 'an overwhelming blow had been struck and both sides knew it'. All that Earl Lloyd George could find to say about this splendid victory was : 'Who remembers the name now? (Try it on one of your friends.)' A wiser reflection is that of the Australian Official Historian, who invites his readers to view the prospects as they appeared on this day, and ask : 'In view of the results of three step-by-step blows, what will be the result of three more in the next fortnight?'

No one will ever know the answer, for at this juncture, the rain came down again, turning the battlefield into a 'porridge of mud'. The whole area now became a mass of waterlogged shell-holes; the streams were blocked and flooded, the drainage system was completely destroyed. Not even the Anzacs, tired after their three victories, nor the weary Imperial divisions which had sustained the brunt of all the fighting, could overcome this obstacle in the torrential, ice-cold, obliterating rain of October 1917. The Battle of Poelcappelle on October 9th and the First Battle of Passchendaele on the 12th petered out in the mud. 'Most gratifying,' noted Crown Prince Rupprecht, the German Army Group Commander, 'rain : our most effective ally.' 'When Plumer consulted me', wrote Birdwood, 'I had to advise against any further advance.' 'I told Haig more than once that it was futile to carry on the attack in mud and rain,' General Gough told the present writer. It is around the continuation, nevertheless, of the battle for a whole month longer that the sharpest controversy has raged. Why did Haig go on ?

There were two reasons for this decision : the first of them is undeniable to anyone who has seen the ground. On October 31st, when the operation was evidently bogged and criticism was mounting, General Kiggell, Haig's Chief of Staff, came to Sir Henry Wilson and 'pleaded that in another eight days Douglas Haig would take enough of the Passchendaele

Ridge to make himself secure for the winter, and that this operation ought not to be stopped'. The wide, bare slopes before Passchendaele look sinister enough today; to halt the Army on them for the winter, under the full observation of the enemy and in the conditions of October 1917, was unthinkable. Passchendaele, important not as a place-name but as a piece of commanding ground, was taken by the Canadians on November 6th and the battle ended four days later.

The other reason for Haig's perseverance was his continuing anxiety about the French. General Charteris, in his biography of Earl Haig, has recorded that the late Field-Marshal, commenting on Mr. Winston Churchill's criticism of this battle, 'added that no one except himself could know of the constant appeals that had been made to him by the French leaders to continue his attack and prevent dangerous developments on the French front, wherever any . . . cessation of the British pressure on the Germans was suggested'. General Gough, whose own reputation was closely concerned with these events, fully accepts this view: 'Haig was strongly urged during all this time to keep up the full weight of his attack, however unpromising the results looked, by Pétain. . . .' Sir John Davidson made this a main defence of Haig's strategy. General Birdwood, also closely concerned, has written that Haig achieved his 'strategic object. The immense and unremitting strain imposed on the Germans had riveted their main forces to the soil of Flanders so that they were unable to send troops south to attack the French.'

The difficulty is that Haig's diary for this period does not contain entries supporting the view that he was markedly influenced by the French appeals. This is a case where the whole truth will probably remain elusive. This writer's opinion is that Haig was certainly worried about the French—as a matter of fact he was always worried about them, as diary entries as early as 1914 demonstrate—and after the information imparted to him earlier he had come to the settled conclusion that his Army must bear the brunt of all fighting in the West in 1917. But that, in itself, is not a sufficient reason for floundering forward through the swamps of Ypres. This direction was forced on him by the necessity of reaching a reasonable winter line. Hindsight tells us now that the French would have been much better supported by saving the men and guns to put real weight behind the brilliant tank assault at Cambrai on November 20th. The final tragedy of 'Third Ypres' was the repulse at Cambrai due to weariness and insufficient reserves.

What was the final balance-sheet? Let us consider the results in relation to the purposes already stated. First, the Channel Ports were certainly a shade more secure; secondly, the Salient had been enlarged and the constriction of the Army lessened, though there had been no breakout; thirdly, the German submarine bases had not even been glimpsed—Passchendaele is only six miles from Ypres—and in fact the submarine menace was overcome without the Army's aid; fourthly, a heavy and damaging blow had, indeed, been struck at the enemy, although the final line reached represented only a portion of the first objective and no exploitable penetration had been effected.

Yet the most important result was, in terms of the

original planning, a by-product. The battle was not fought to save the French Army; but it did save the French nevertheless. At any time during this period a heavy German onslaught on the French could have brought total disaster to the Allies. While the British offensive continued, the enemy were unable to strike such a blow, and under Pétain's careful nursing, the French Army revived sufficiently to be able to stage a useful small offensive of its own at Verdun in August, and to play a vital part in the battles of 1918.[7]

The British casualties from July 31st to November 21st are given by the Official History as 244,897.[8] This works out at an average of just over 2,300 per day, compared with an average of over 3,000 per day on the Somme in 1916, over 2,400 per day at Cambrai later, and over 5,300 per day, according to some accounts, in the French Army in all the fighting of 1914. German casualties cannot be exactly computed, but the British Official Historian, after reasoned analysis, places them at approximately 300,000. Certainly the German accounts dwell on the severity of their losses; their Official History sums up: 'The offensive had protected the French against fresh German attacks, and thereby procured them time to re-consolidate their badly shattered troops. . . . But, above all, the battle had led to an excessive expenditure of German forces. The casualties were so great that they could no longer be covered. . . .' The German official monograph *Flandern* goes even further: 'In the year 1918 it turned out that their success definitely contributed to the result that the war ended in favour of the Allies; but when the Flanders battle was broken off they had no inducement to look on it as decisive.' And the Chief of Staff of the Fourth German Army wrote : 'The Flanders battle consumed the German strength to such a degree that the harm done could no longer be repaired.'

It was not, in fact, the casualties that represented the worst aspect of the battle from the British point of view; it was, first, the vast depression of the human spirit in this hideous arena, summed up by Sir Philip Gibbs, then a War Correspondent, and confirmed by many others : 'For the first time the British Army lost its spirit of optimism.' The second grave result was the further deterioration of relations between G.H.Q. and the British Government. As the offensive floundered in the Flanders mud, the Prime Minister and the Commander-in-Chief moved further apart. Haig felt that he had been let down and would discuss none of his problems openly with the Premier; Lloyd George was sure that he was being deceived by a military clique. He turned away from his responsible advisers to advisers without responsibility. He could not pluck up the political courage either to sack the men he distrusted or to resign himself, nor could he comes to terms with them; instead he sought again to weaken them by indirect means. His most effective weapon was to withhold reinforcements, which he did. One result was the Cambrai fiasco in November 1917; another was the collapse of the Fifth Army in March 1918. A third could easily have been the loss of the War.

Were there any alternatives to 'Third Ypres'? The Lloyd George school has put forward two strategic alternatives : first, there was the system, advocated by

Pétain, of staging small, careful, economical, local attacks until American man-power could be made effective.[9] We know a lot more about Pétain now than Lloyd George did when he compiled his memoirs. But, to be fair, Pétain was in a dilemma at the time. He could not freely divulge the condition of his Army, but at the same time he dared not commit it to large ventures. He had to find a philosophy of inactivity, and, of course, he was just the man to do this. He did not intend that this policy should apply to the British Army. The Germans, however, were never alarmed by Pétain's limited offensives, skilful and successful though they were. The battle against the British, on the other hand, became their 'greatest martyrdom of the war'.

Lloyd George's favourite idea was a knock-out blow against Austria on the Italian front, which he still believed to be viable. G.H.Q.'s answer to this never varied; the enemy held the interior lines and would always be able to defend them more easily than we could maintain an attack, and the more we stretched our communications, the harder our task would become. In the light of what was achieved by only a small reinforcement of German divisions at Caporetto, it is not difficult to envisage the battle we would have had to fight on the Carso against the full weight of their reserves, or what might have happened in France while our strength was being deployed on the Adriatic. So the strategic alternatives to the British offensive were never real and, given the submarine menace, there was never any doubt that it would have to be launched in Flanders.

The tactical alternative, which could have made the story read very differently, was not even canvassed because it lay in the future, in a revolution of warfare. It was the surprise element reintroduced by mechanisation which was to be essayed at Cambrai, perfected on the Somme, and brought to fruition at Amiens on August 8th, 1918.

PART II—AMIENS

If Passchendaele is the symbol of everything going wrong, Amiens is the symbol of everything coming right. If Passchendaele was an epic of drawn-out endurance, Amiens was quick surgery. Passchendaele was the last attempt of the British Army to break the enemy by sheer weight and persistence; Amiens was the battle of skill and mechanical superiority. Under Plumer, the science of applied weight, particularly weight of artillery, was brought to a very high pitch; but even at its most successful, this strategy of infinite preparation and strictly limited advance looks clumsy and antiquated beside the new science of surprise and movement which was worked out under Rawlinson on the Somme in 1918.

Ypres and the Somme were the two main battlefields of the British Armies during the First World War. On both of them the slaughter of British soldiers, the suffering, the resolution, and the heroism were prodigious. Ypres, in spite of the tactical difficulties presented by the famous Salient and the horrors of the notorious Flanders mud, was always regarded as the 'natural' place for our armies to fight in, partly for historical reasons because of the proximity of the Channel Ports, but partly also because of its remoteness from the French. Close co-operation between the two Allies rarely worked well, and it was largely for this reason that the Somme was never greatly favoured. There was a sounder strategic reason too. The first Battle of the Somme, in 1916, was fought at the insistence of Joffre. It had, says the British Official Historian, 'no strategic object except attrition'. The area was chosen solely because it contained the junction of the French and British Armies; this, in the French view, would force the reluctant British to put all their strength into the fight. Their final casualty list of 415,000 indicates that they did so. In 1917, with the demoralised French Army playing a mainly passive role after the Nivelle offensive, and the Flanders campaign requiring every available man and gun, the British were able to concentrate their efforts to the north. But at the end of the year's fighting the French raised once more their familiar demand for the British to take over more of the front. Haig was forced to agree, with the result that a weakened Fifth Army found itself stretched along an untenable line covering the ill-omened Somme area. Here it was caught by the great German attack of March 21st, and flung back some forty miles across the devastated battle area of 1916 to the very outskirts of Amiens.

Situated at the hinge of the two Allied Armies, this big rail centre now assumed a vital significance. It was to prevent the fall of Amiens that Foch was appointed Generalissimo at Haig's instigation. The necessity of freeing it once and for all from the enemy's menaces needed no stating. The strategy of counter-attacking on the Somme was equally obvious to Foch and to Haig; but was it tactically feasible? The equally compelling though more complicated strategic necessities at Ypres had been baulked by weather, ground and the enemy's defensive system. The familiar but bitter lesson was that strategy ignores tactics at its peril. The British Army, gravely weakened after the two great German offensives against it on the Somme on March 21st, and on the Lys on April 9th—two months during which its casualties exceeded those of four months at Passchendaele—and with its ranks only with difficulty being maintained by drafts of boys and Category 'B' men, did not appear to be the most promising tactical instrument to hand for a decisive blow. Yet its commander, Field-Marshal Sir Douglas Haig, never lost faith in it. He was among the first to see an opportunity for a counter-attack, and the optimism which had been a fault in him at other times was now to be justified.

The Battle of Amiens is like the bursting through of suppressed, frustrated forces. The unshakable persistence of the British High Command, the steadily acquired skills of the intermediate commands, the soldierly qualities of endurance and of dash (so often squandered), the technical and mechanical advances, the huge material product of a nation only belatedly mobilised, all at last were to come together and achieve a great result.

The first sign of this coming together was witnessed on April 25th, the third anniversary of Anzac Day,

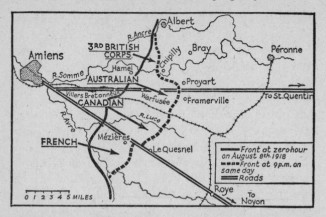

when the Australian recapture of the ruined red-brick commune of Villers Bretonneux marked definitively the high-tide line of the German advance towards Amiens. Two days previously, as the enemy swept through the mist of early morning towards the city whose cathedral spire had been their target for so long, it was observed that they were accompanied by three huge square forms—German tanks. The British infantry gave way before them; two 'female' British tanks, armed only with machine-guns, were knocked out; and then a third British tank, a 'male' with six-pounders, under Lieutenant Mitchell of the 1st Tank Battalion, knocked out one of the Germans, whereupon the other two retired. This was the first tank *versus* tank battle in history. More immediately significant, taken in conjunction with a brilliant spoiling action against a German build-up by seven Whippet tanks of the 3rd Battalion on the same day, it presaged the co-operation of tanks and Australian infantry, under General Rawlin-

son, which was to be a main feature of the fighting
that was to follow on the Somme.

What immediately followed, however, was the continuation of the great German offensives. On the day
after Villers Bretonneux was retaken, Kemmel Hill was
lost. The Lys front was stabilised only by a tremendous
effort on the part of both the British and the French.
On May 27th, the Germans switched the direction of
their onslaught southward against the French front,
overwhelming more British troops (who had been sent
to recuperate on a 'quiet sector') in their deep penetration between Soissons and Rheims. On June 9th, a
second prong of this attack thrust forward in the direction of Compiègne, and the two attacks together
accounted for some 70,000 prisoners and 830 guns.

It was against the background of these ominous
thunders that Sir Douglas Haig, in all his imperturbability of spirit, which some have called obtuseness and
some have called callousness but which was, in fact, no
more than the composure of a man who is sure of his
professional qualifications and acts upon them without
stint or deviation, conceived the counter-stroke that
was to mark the turning of the War. His diary tersely
records on May 17th, ten days before the Germans
began their assault against the French on the Aisne : 'I
told Rawlinson to begin studying in conjunction with
General Debeney [Commander of the neighbouring
First French Army] the question of an attack eastwards
from Villers Bretonneux in combination with an attack
from the French front south of Roye. I gave him
details of the scheme.' Two months were to pass before
Haig communicated his ideas to Foch, and almost

three before they could be put into practice.[10] For the greater part of these three months such ideas would have seemed to contain the ring of lunacy, but all the time Rawlinson and his subordinates were progressing steadily with their preparations, assembling the properties and working out the moves of the great drama.

One, in particular, of these subordinates was to play a major role, to make a distinctive contribution. This was the new commander of the Australian Army Corps, now at last about to assemble all its five divisions to fight together in one formation on one battlefield for the first time—Lieutenant-General Sir John Monash. General Monash is one British Commander of the First World War who leaves one in no doubt that he would have been equally at home in the Second.

Certainly he stood apart from the all 'Imperial' officers with whom he served. A Jew, a civil engineer by profession, a part-time, 'Saturday-afternoon' soldier, he brought to the profession of war a seriousness and efficiency that was only rarely matched by the Regular professional soldiers. War, above all, was serious to him. One of his Staff Officers has told the present writer : 'He treated war as a business; I don't believe he thought about anything during the War except winning the War.' He lacked the affability that long regimental experience confers on the good Regular officer in his relations with other ranks; he lacked the sociability that mess life stimulates; he was not a front-line soldier. He made up for this in brain-power, organisation and relentlessness of purpose. In that war, of which the martyred infantryman has become the

symbol, Monash's views on the role of infantry contain
the core of his thinking, the deepest reason for his success, and the reason for the total confidence that his
men placed in him.

'I had formed the theory', he wrote, 'that the true
role of the infantry was not to expend itself upon
heroic physical effort, not to wither away under
merciless machine-gun fire, nor to impale itself on
hostile bayonets, nor to tear itself to pieces in hostile
entanglements . . . but on the contrary, to advance
under the maximum possible protection of the maximum possible array of mechanical resources, in the
form of guns, machine-guns, tanks, mortars, and
aeroplanes; to advance with as little impediment as
possible; to be relieved as far as possible of the
obligation to *fight* their way forward; to march
resolutely, regardless of the din and tumult of battle
to the appointed goal, and there to hold and defend
the territory gained; and to gather, in the form of
prisoners, guns, and stores, the fruits of victory.'

The first indication of what this theory could mean
in practice was seen at the battle of Le Hamel on July
4th. This was a small-scale, tidying-up operation,
whose object was to clear the enemy out of an awk-
ward salient between Villers Bretonneux and the
Somme and to win further observation to the eastward
while denying to the enemy a valuable view into our
back areas. The troops concerned were some ten battalions of the 4th Australian Division, with sixty Mark
V tanks and four supply tanks of the 5th Tank
Brigade. Four companies of American infantry were

also to make their first offensive appearance on the British front. There was strong artillery support but no preliminary preparation by the guns.

This was not a complete novelty but was still enough of a rarity; there were, however, other innovations even more important. The tanks were carefully trained beforehand in co-operation with the Australian infantry, who ever since Bullecourt in April 1917, and the subsequent spectacle of tanks hopelessly bogged in the mud of Flanders, had been especially sceptical of their value. Now each infantry company learned to know its supporting tanks individually. General Monash believed that the tanks could go forward beside the infantry immediately behind the barrage. There were many who doubted, pointing out the risk of the lofty tank-frames being hit by our own shells. But the thing was tried and proved entirely successful. The four carrier tanks took forward loads equal to those of a bearer party 1,250 strong. Aircraft distributed 100,000 rounds of ammunition to the machine-gunners as they occupied their new positions—the first use of an air-lift of supplies on a field of battle. Surprise was cultivated throughout.

But more important than all this was the significance that Monash attached to his battle-plan. 'A perfected modern battle-plan', he wrote, 'is like nothing so much as a score for an orchestral composition. . . .' The stress is on the word 'perfected'. He introduced now the system that was to become standard in the Australian Corps for the rest of the War :

'Although completely written orders were invari-

ably prepared and issued . . . very great importance was attached to the holding of conferences, at
which were assembled every one of the senior commanders and heads of departments concerned in the
impending operation. At these I personally explained every detail of the plan, and assured myself
that *all present applied an identical interpretation*
. . . the battle plan having been thus crystallised,
*no subsequent alterations were permissible, under
any circumstances,* no matter how tempting.'[11]

To this last point he attached the very greatest importance.

His firmness on it was not long in being put to the
test. For 'political' reasons, at the last moment, Sir
Douglas Haig ordered Rawlinson to withdraw the
American contingent. But each American platoon had
its special function in Monash's plan : 'I well knew
that . . . the withdrawal of those Americans would
result in untold confusion . . . so I resolved to take a
firm stand and press my views as strongly as I dared;
for even a corps commander must use circumspection
when presuming to argue with an army commander.'
Circumspect or not, Monash in effect told Rawlinson :
'No Americans, no battle.' Rawlinson agreed to leave
the Americans in, and Haig readily assented to his
decision when the case was put to him. Monash comments : 'It appeared to me at the time that great issues
had hung for an hour or so upon the chance of my
being able to carry my point.'

Great issues indeed had hung, for the battle that
followed was an unqualified success, all over in 93

minutes. The Australians lost 51 officers and 724 other ranks, the Americans six officers and 128 enlisted men, the tanks had three machines damaged and 13 men wounded; 41 German officers, 1,431 other ranks, two field guns, 26 trench mortars, and 171 machine-guns were captured. It was a clear sign : there was no mistaking what it portended. But above all it vindicated and established this method of making war, whose novelty may seen questionable to the veterans of the Second World War, but which, in 1918, was a revolution :

> 'In a well-planned battle . . .' says Monash, 'nothing happens, *nothing can happen,* except the regular progress of the advance according to the plan arranged. . . . It is for this reason that no stirring accounts exist of . . . great set-pieces. . . . They will never be written, for there is no material on which to base them. The story of what did take place on the day of battle *would be a mere paraphrase of the battle orders* prescribing all that was to take place.'[12]

This language has, indeed, a familiar ring to the generation that knew Montgomery. But the immediate point is that Monash's plan was published as a Staff brochure by G.H.Q., and his method was adopted for the whole Fourth Army in the larger attack that was now about to be launched.

For this large attack, the Battle of Amiens, General Rawlinson had four Army Corps (fifteen infantry divisions and three cavalry divisions) available. His artillery amounted to 2,070 guns and howitzers, one field

piece to every twenty-nine yards of front, one heavy to
every fifty-nine yards. At the peak of the Passchendaele fighting the density of artillery had been as much
as one piece per 5.2 yards. It was not artillery that
Rawlinson depended on to win this battle; it was the
weapon of surprise—the tank. The Fourth Army had
under command no less than 534 tanks (compared with
476 at Cambrai), consisting of 342 of the new and
excellent Mark Vs, 72 Whippets and 120 supply tanks.
Just under 800 aircraft completed the formidable
mechanical array at Rawlinson's disposal. On his
right the First French Army, under General Debeney,
was placed by Foch under Sir Douglas Haig's orders
to ensure cohesion.

But important as this massing of material strength
was, it was completely overshadowed by the devotion
to surprise which permeated every part of the Fourth
Army plan. There had been huge material endeavours
before and they had often come to nothing; surprise
had been much neglected in that war[13] yet it had
always produced results. Now it was to be everything.
In all details the Fourth Army staff were meticulous :
secrecy was dinned into all ranks; deception was prac-
tised in every possible way. Tremendous care was taken
with the registration of new batteries; all forward movement of troops or vehicles after August 1st was done
by night; aeroplanes flew over the whole area to report
on anything that might be seen by the enemy and
appear to him suspicious. But the prodigies of secret
preparation were the introduction into the area of two
large formations, the presence of either which would,
if perceived, have told the enemy beyond any doubt

what was afoot—the Cavalry Corps and the Canadian Corps. With the cavalry, coming out of reserve, the problem was one entirely of concealment—difficult enough with their long horse-lines and large forage dumps in the empty uplands of the Somme; with the Canadians, already identified on the front of the First Army, the problem was even more complex. Deception on the grand scale would be required.

The performance that followed has a sound about it of the preparations for Alamein and the D-Day ruses. It was worked out by the staff of the Fourth Army; the hand of their wily commander, General Rawlinson, was obviously present. At Rawlinson's request, two Canadian battalions, with two casualty clearing stations and the wireless section, were transferred from First Army to Second Army and put into the line opposite Kemmel Hill. This was an excellent feint, for the Canadians had so far not been engaged in any of the heavy fighting of the year; what was more likely than for the Germans to believe that this first-rate fighting unit would be used to retake the key position of the northern front? The Canadians were soon identified there and this evidence, in conjunction with greatly increased air and wireless activity in the First and Second Army zones, completely deceived the enemy. It was almost a week before they realised that they had 'lost' the Canadians, and by then the big battle was on the point of opening.

To cover the arrival of the 100,000-strong Canadian Corps in the Fourth Army area a further ruse was adopted, of the same doubly significant order. It was decided to keep the Canadians out of the line until the

very eve of the attack in order to prevent identification.
The sector they were to occupy ran some 7,000 yards
south of Villers Bretonneux, in the area of the First
French Army. This portion of the front was now taken
over by the Australian Corps—a manœuvre which
suggested the exact opposite of what was intended. It
could only have been construed as a freeing of French
troops for offensive action, and an anticipation of
quiescence by the Australians. Not that these aggressive, active soldiers were ever particularly quiescent. In
order for them to take over this new sector, their own
left flank near Morlancourt was relieved on July 30th
by the British 3rd Corps. On their last night in this
sector, the Australians performed one more successful
act of what they dryly termed 'peaceful penetration'
—a mode of behaviour which had helped to keep this
whole front fluid since April. 'Peaceful penetration'
meant frequent, furious, damaging, murderous raids :
this one netted three officers, 135 other ranks, thirty-six
machine-guns, and two trench mortars. The Australians came away from Morlancourt well pleased with
themselves, but the anger they had stirred up was to
have a mischievous effect on the big plan.

And now the plan was well advanced. On July 28th
Foch issued his directive for the operation : on August
3rd he met Sir Douglas Haig to confirm the date and
final details. On August 5th Haig met Rawlinson and
General Debeney, with Lieutenant-General Kavanagh,
commanding the Cavalry Corps. He took this opportunity, in conformance with Foch's ideas, to revise
parts of the Fourth Army plan which he thought to be
too conservative, and to impress on those present the

need for a deep advance, without any delay for the consolidation that was regarded as a statutory phase of any attack. How many times had G.H.Q. revised the plans of local commanders in this sense! How many times had the effect of the revision been greater loss of life with no compensating gain! This time, at last, and for the rest of the War, Haig's vision of victory within grasp was to be proved true.

And yet, as though to demonstrate once more the chanciness of war, even with the most careful planning, the most original thinking, the completest surprise, the following day brought an ugly shock. Reacting, after a week of preparation, to the Australian frolic of July 29th, the Germans fell upon the front of the British 3rd Corps, north of the Somme, with a powerful assault division, newly arrived in the area. They caught the 58th and 18th Divisions in the middle of relief and quickly penetrated to a depth of some 800 yards, taking over 200 prisoners. British line divisions were neither morally nor materially the equal of the Dominion divisions at this period. Reduced to only nine battalions by the reorganisation at the beginning of the year, weakened by their efforts during the great retreat, and mostly below establishment, they were now feeling the disadvantage of the voluntary system, which had allowed Kitchener to scoop the best of the nation into his 'New Armies', leaving a relatively un-leavened mass when conscription was at last applied. There was no lack of bravery, but skill and spirit were often wanting. This truth was to be vividly demon-strated by force of contrast during the next few days. Meanwhile, the weakest element of the Fourth Army

—3rd Corps—was faced with the hardest task, for instead of resting on the eve of the great attack, it had to spend its energy on recovering this lost ground and then pass immediately into the main offensive.

The real question, however, was whether this German blow had been truly a local counter-manœuvre or whether it indicated a larger awareness of what was coming. The anxious staffs concluded that this was not the case. G.H.Q. formally named August 8th as 'the Day', and Rawlinson and Debeney settled their zero hours: for the British, 4.20 a.m.—just before first light; for the French, forty-five minutes later, since they would not be using tanks and required a short preparatory barrage. On the German side, the front-line troops were digesting Ludendorff's latest order of the day, dated August 4th, and opening with these words: 'I am under the impression that, in many quarters, the possibility of an enemy offensive is viewed with a certain degree of apprehension. There is nothing to justify this apprehension, provided our troops are vigilant and do their duty . . . we should wish for nothing better than to see the enemy launch an offensive, which can but hasten the disintegration of his forces. . . .' Shortly afterwards he drew up a more anxious paper, dwelling on the necessity for defence in depth to guard against surprise, but by the time it arrived the soldiers it was meant to instruct were mostly on their way to the Fourth Army's prisoner-of-war cages.

The day of August 8th opened with dense mist. On some parts of the front the maximum visibility was no more than ten feet. When the mist cleared a day of brilliant sunshine followed. At last the weather, which had so fatally betrayed the British Army a year before, changed sides, and the very conditions which had so much assisted the German offensive of March 21st were now to operate entirely in our favour. The rolling barrage came down with crackling precision, and the long lines of tanks and infantry swept forward through the misty half-light, Canadians on the right, Australians in the centre, 3rd Corps on the left. Not until the mist cleared could they actually see the effect they were producing, but they began to have the 'feel' of it straight away. Except on one sector there were no checks, no untoward halts. The forward movement, necessarily slow in the mist, continued steadily; the supports, coming up behind, never collided with the front divisions, but passed through them dead on time and without a hitch. By seven o'clock the Australians were all on their first objective; by half past ten on their second; by eleven o'clock the Canadians were up alongside. As the mists cleared and the sun burst through at about this time, a remarkable sight was seen in the wide spaces of the centre of the field :

'the whole Santerre plateau seen from the air was dotted with parties of infantry, field artillery, and tanks moving forward. Staff officers were galloping about, many riding horses in battle for the first time. . . . Indeed, at this stage there was more noise of movement than of firing, as the heavy batteries . . . were no longer in action; for the infantry had gone so far that it was no longer possible for them to shoot. . . . No enemy guns seemed to be firing and no co-ordinated defence was apparent. . . .'[14]

By 1.30 p.m. the main fighting was over. The Australians had occupied all their objectives, except on their extreme flanks where their neighbours were behind them; the Canadians had advanced almost eight miles.

It had been a sensational day but not devoid of hazards. By common consent the tanks had done marvels. Against German infantry and machine-guns they had proved irresistible, and countless infantry lives had been saved by their action. The German artillery, on the other hand, had not suffered the loss of morale that the year's high casualties had brought about in the infantry. They stuck to their guns, often shooting at tanks at point-blank range. Ten tanks of the 1st Battalion attacked Le Quesnel in the Canadian sector; nine were set on fire by direct hits from field guns at seventy yards. A line of twelve tanks, topping the crest of a rise which marked their starting line with the 5th Australian Division, had six knocked out immediately by field guns at a range of half a mile, another immediately afterwards, and three more shortly after that. Collaboration between the Whippets and the cavalry, of which much had been expected, proved an illusion. On the other hand, the Whippets themselves were most successful, outflanking batteries, supporting patrols, mopping up, and many of them experiencing adventures similar to, though it would scarcely be possible to equal, those of the legendary tank 'Musical Box'. The armoured cars of the 17th Battalion, once the long straight Roman road which bisects the battlefield was cleared, plunged deep into the German back areas, shooting up infantry and transport and capturing a corps staff.

In the centre victory was complete. The Canadians captured 114 officers, 4,919 other ranks, 161 guns and uncounted hundreds of machine-guns and mortars; their losses were about 3,500. The Australians captured 183 officers, 7,742 other ranks, 173 guns and hundreds of smaller trophies. Their losses were under 3,000. Only on the flanks was there any setback. The 3rd Corps, after a difficult day on the 7th, trying to win back its lost ground, spent a bad night against an alert enemy. There was much German shelling, particularly with gas, which caused many casualties. Surprise was out of the question; the enemy were as strong as the attackers; the ground steep and well wooded, was much more difficult than the smooth terrain of the centre. The main objective of the Corps was the Chipilly spur, thrusting its promontory into the Somme which is here compelled to make a wide southward bend. Unless taken, this spur would prove a serious handicap to the left of the Australian advance; but to take it proved beyond the powers of the 58th Division. 3rd Corps was not able to progress beyond its first objective, with the result that the advancing Australians were caught in enfilade by machine-guns and field artillery sited on the spur. They suffered their most serious casualties and their only failure at this point.

When every allowance is made for the special conditions that applied to the 3rd Corps front, there remains a contrast between the performance of these divisions and that of the Dominion troops so marked that a further explanation has to be sought. The British Official Historian makes this comment: '. . . there was not only a shortage of experienced officers and non-commissioned officers, but the ranks of the infantry units had been filled up with young recruits from home. These convalescent divisions had not entered with great enthusiasm on the hard task of preparing a field of battle . . . the willing co-operation usually exhibited before an attack was absent.' In other words, after four years of war, the British Army was showing signs of war-weariness that did not, so far, affect the soldiers of the younger nations who had spent less time on the Western Front.

Nor was this feeling confined to the British. In the French sector, where the going was very much easier, the absence of 'push' was even more marked. General Debeney's instructions to his Army had been vehement in the French manner :

> '. . . the attacks will be conducted with but one pre-occupation, to achieve the greatest rapidity in a succession of forward bounds. . . . Alignment is not to be sought; it is forbidden to wait for neighbouring divisions . . . the attacks will be pushed on and continued until night; from the very first day the troops must go "very far".'

This did not occur. Starting three-quarters of an hour after the Canadians, whose advance naturally eased their progress on the left, the French moved so deliberately that when the Canadian line halted, it was five hours before the French came up abreast of them.

General Debeney was found by Sir Douglas Haig during the afternoon 'almost in tears because three battalions of his Colonial infantry had bolted before a German machine-gun'. Making all due allowance for Haig's sardonic view of his allies, it is clear that the First French Army was not performing well. The French had shown great fire in their counter-attack at Soissons in July under Mangin. They were to show it again and again before the War ended. But Debeney was no Mangin, and the French Army in 1918 was not of the same calibre as the fine troops who had been squandered in 1915 and 1916.

But whatever deficiencies may have appeared in the French ranks and in the line divisions of the British Army, they were nothing to those exposed in the German Army. The German Official Monograph on the battle sums up the day from the enemy's point of view :

'As the sun set on August 8th on the battlefield the greatest defeat which the German Army had suffered since the beginning of the war was an accomplished fact. The position divisions between the Avre and the Somme which had been struck by the enemy attack were nearly completely annihilated. The troops in the front line north of the Somme had also suffered seriously, as also the reserve divisions thrown into the battle in the course of the day. The total loss of the formations employed in the *Second Army* area is estimated at 650 to 700 officers and 26,000 to 27,000 other ranks. More than 400 guns, besides a huge number of machine-guns, trench mortars, and other war material had been lost. . . . More than two-thirds of the total loss had surrendered as prisoners.'

Ludendorff wrote : 'August 8th was the black day of the German Army in the history of the war. This was the worst experience I had to go through . . . our losses had reached such proportions that the Supreme Command was faced with the necessity of having to disband a series of divisions. . . . August 8th made things clear for both army commands, both for the German and for that of the enemy.'

The attack continued on the following day, but the initial impetus could not be regained. Only 145 tanks were fit for action; German reserves were arriving on the scene; many of the British troops were tired after their great exertions. Yet there is a sense of wasted opportunities on the 9th : the only notable gain of the day was the capture of the Chipilly spur by an American unit, the 131st Regiment, attached to 3rd Corps. General Monash records his disappointment at the semi-defensive orders given to his Corps: 'I should have welcomed an order to push on . . . in open warfare formation . . . the order stood, however. . . .' There can be little doubt that both on this day and the next the British Fourth Army found it difficult to make the adjustment to the new conditions of open warfare and movement created by their own success on the 8th. Rawlinson, not unnaturally, feared the now-familiar German tactics of retirement and counter-attack which had brought to nothing the success at Cambrai, and felt it necessary to prepare some defensive positions against such an eventuality. As for the French, the combined exhortations of Foch, Haig and Debeney could not re-instil in their divisions the offensive spirit that so many failures had undermined. On August 10th the intervention of the French Third Army, on the right of the First, helped to pull that wing of the battle forward, but in general the advance that day was small. German resistance was stiffening and, worse still, the Allies were now approaching the old battlefields of 1916 with their maze of trenches, their jungles of wire, and their concrete fortifications. This ground was wholly unsuitable even for heavy tanks, let alone the Whippets and the cavalry. A change of plan was evidently required.

Once again it was Haig who, in effect, took strategic charge of the operations, just as it was he who had originated them far back in May. Foch, ardent and aggressive as ever, was all for pushing on, and indeed, issued instructions in that sense. But Haig had already seen that this course might be impossible, and had already begun preparations for a new blow on the front of the British Third Army. Now he extended these to the fronts of the First and Second Armies also. For a day Foch's persistence overbore Haig, who was constrained to continue his pressure on Rawlinson. But the latter, remembering no doubt the ordeal that his Army had gone through on these very battlefields in 1916, resisted the pressure strongly. The Official Historian informs us that he even said to Haig: 'Who commands the British Army, you or Foch?' The slight advances and small captures of 10th August decided Haig. The following day he returned to his arguments against the Generalissimo's plans, and won Foch over to an agreement to switch the main operation northward from the front of the Fourth Army to that of the Third. It was some days before Foch could bring himself to make this change of plan formal, but he generously acknowledged why he did so: 'I definitely came around to the opinion of Field-Marshal Sir Douglas Haig. . . .' And so the Army was spared a second Somme, but instead went on to a second victory at Albert ten days later.

This date, August 11th, was in its way as decisive as the 8th. German morale was now unmistakably waning and the infection was reaching the support divisions arriving on the battlefield. The German *38th Division,* coming up, met 'drunken Bavarians who shouted to the *94th Regiment*: "What do you war-prolongers want? If the enemy were only on the Rhine—the war would then be over!" ' Other retreating troops shouted to the *263rd Reserve Regiment*: 'We thought that we had set the thing going, now you asses are corking up the hole again.' Ludendorff, at a meeting of the High Command with the Kaiser on this day, reported 'that the warlike spirit of some of the divisions left a good deal to be desired . . . when the Kaiser and Crown Prince suggested that too much had been asked of the troops, Ludendorff replied that the collapse of the *Second Army* on August 8th could not be accounted for by the divisions being over-tired. He offered his resignation, but it was not accepted.' It was at this same meeting, on August 11th, that the Kaiser uttered these words: .

'I see that we must strike a balance. We have nearly reached the limit of our powers of resistance. The war must be ended.'

This was the victory. This was the fruit of all the courage, all the preparation, all the skill in planning, all the dash in battle. This cancelled out all the set-backs. This, at last, meant the justification of the sacrifices over the years. For what this meant was, as the Official Historian says, that 'the collapse of Germany began not in the Navy, not in the Homeland, not in any of the sideshows, but on the Western Front in consequence of defeat in the field'.

NOTES

1. I would now rephrase this sentence to read : 'Haig, who all through 1916 had wished to make the main British effort in Flanders, was delighted when Joffre belatedly came round to his view.'

2. In May 1917 the British Government insisted that Haig should obtain explicit assurances from General Pétain, the new French C.-in-C., that his armies would, indeed, support the British with major operations. These assurances were procured at the Amiens conference on May 18th.

3. The Vimy Ridge was captured by the Canadian Corps, belonging to General Horne's First Army.

4. British casualties for this battle were 17,000; German, 25,000.

5. The exact contrary; see note 2.

6. It is easy to be misled by words. Haig says : 'put the whole situation . . . before me and conceal nothing'. But did Debeney, in fact, do so? The more carefully one reads Haig's diary, the more weight one is forced to

attach to the next part of the quote; Haig was really only conscious of the dropping of the June attack, and subsequently showed much irritation at the delaying of a promised July attack until August. Nothing in his diary supports the view that he thought the French had been 'knocked out'.

7. I do not now entirely agree with this. The recuperation of the French Army was of obvious value. But I now believe that 'the most important result' of the battle was the damage done to the Germans.

8. It is odd that so much discussion should have raged about this figure; it is the one submitted to the Supreme War Council of the Allies by the British Section of the Military Representatives on February 25th, 1918. It is thus, as the Official Historian says, a contemporary figure, 'not "an elaborate effort to gerrymander the casualty returns" '. The Supreme War Council was, in effect, a 'rival concern' to British G.H.Q., and would closely scrutinise every return coming from Haig's headquarters. At that time the Supreme War Council was advocating a considerable extension of the British Front, and the allocation of British divisions to a central Allied Reserve. Both these demands were being determinedly resisted by Haig and his Staff; in self-defence, therefore, they would be tempted to state their casualties in the last great battle as high as possible, in order to avert the evils which threatened them.

9. It is worth remembering, when this 'wait for America' theory is advanced, that the first American intervention on the field of battle in considerable strength was the Battle of St. Mihiel on September 26th, 1918— only six weeks before the War ended.

10. This is quite incorrect. I was misled here by Robert Blake's *The Private Papers of Douglas Haig 1914-1919* (London:Eyre & Spottiswoode, 1952). Blake,

who had to edit severely, has no entry between May 11th and May 17th. Not until I read the full text of Haig's diary did I take due note of what Duff Cooper had already reproduced in his *Haig* (London : Faber, 1935), an entry on May 16th which reads :

'Foch also explained to me an offensive project which he wishes to carry out if the enemy does not launch his big attack within the next few weeks. I agreed with his general plan, and said I would study my share of the undertaking and let him know. But he must not write his plan or let the French Commanders talk about it. Success will depend mainly on secrecy.'

The next day Haig gave Rawlinson his cue, and then ten days later, the Germans attacked the French on the Aisne. Foch rather lost sight of the Amiens project as the critical weeks of June and July went past, but Haig did not. When the moment was ripe, he reminded Foch of what had been agreed; Foch took up the idea with renewed zest; so Amiens becomes a joint achievement of the two marshals. I submit, however, that after the first moment of inception, it was Haig who played the major part in this great victory.

11, 12. Author's italics.

13. Not so much neglected as well-nigh impossible to achieve. It was only the appearance of tanks which made it possible to abandon the tell-tale long initial bombardments.

14. Official History.

Because of the peculiarities of Britain's role in the War, and the transitions through which it passed—because, in short, of the factors which constituted Lloyd George's dilemma, and which led to his expedients—no leading figure became more controversial than Field-Marshal Earl Haig, O.M., K.T., G.C.B., G.C.V.O., K.C.I.E., who held the appointment of Commander-in-Chief of the British forces on the Western Front from December 19th, 1915, until the end of the War.

When I first began to study the War seriously, about twenty-five years ago, I approached Lord Haig's performance in the spirit which was then becoming fashionable, and which in some quarters remains vigorous today. I thought of him as an unimaginative 'slogger', imbued with absurd and unreal optimism, fatally detached from battlefield realities. This approach caused me to miss most of the valuable points in Duff Cooper's excellent biography, which I read shortly after it appeared. My sheer lack of knowledge of the details and circumstances of the War made it inevitable that I would also fail to see the significance of large portions of Haig's diary, from which Duff Cooper quoted lavishly. It was not until Robert Blake's *Private Papers of Douglas Haig* came out in 1952, by which time I had learnt much, that I was in a condition to review these rashly formed opinions. I then wrote, in a letter to the *New Statesman and Nation*:

'We may not like the psychological basis of Haig's

imperturbability. We may condem the system that
moulded him. But it could not have been a "small"
man who bore that massive responsibility, and
worked out his behaviour by the creed of a world
in whose destruction he himself was taking, un-
wittingly, a major part.'

My studies continued : they kept returning to Haig,
whose career seemed to crystallise so many facets of
the War itself. In 1958, writing in *The Spectator* to
commemorate the 40th anniversary of the events of
1918, which I considered to be 'the year of Haig's
vindication', I said : 'Haig's achievement is solid.' But
I also said, believing it to be true :

> 'On the debit side of Haig's balance sheet, it has
> to be stated that he was no restless seeker after new
> techniques of conducting war. Neither, of course,
> was Wellington. . . . It is impossible not to con-
> nect the slogging matches into which so many of
> Haig's battles developed with his missionary persis-
> tence of purpose. Persistence so often took on the
> features of pure obstinacy, as though Haig had
> accepted the martyrdom of his army and the hazard
> of his own reputation as part of the necessary
> sacrifices upon the altar of the God of victory.'

Further researches, including the reading of the full
text of his diary, and its mass of associated papers, led
me to the very different conclusions which I expressed
in *Douglas Haig: The Educated Soldier* (London :
Hutchinson, 1963). But research into history never
ends; I am already dissatisfied with parts of that

book, wondering whether I have not helped to per-
petuate in it injustices to the man. In particular, I
wonder whether I said enough about that astonishing
sequence of victories which he won in 1918.

For, in the last resort, studies of this kind depend
upon a starting point. For many people, the starting
point of thinking about Haig is the grim casualty list
for the Somme and 'Passchendaele'. Yet this is wrong,
because grim casualty lists were not exceptional in that
war. Every army had them, every general was 'guilty'
in this way; it tells us nothing special about Haig. The
worst of the lot were probably those of the Russians, in
many fearful conflicts; as I have said earlier, 1915
alone is said to have cost them two million men. The
French are reputed to have lost about 800,000 in the
four effective months of 1914 fighting; Ludendorff lost
rather more than that figure in the four months of his
final 1918 offensives.

What *is* exceptional about Haig is the hundred days
of uninterrupted victory by which he did so much to
bring the War to an end. Marshal Foch made no
bones about this contribution; in his introduction to
Haig's Despatches, he inscribed this formidable list :

'*Battle of Amiens,* Aug. 8–13, in which the Fourth
Army took 22,000 prisoners and more than 400
guns.

Battle of Bapaume, Aug. 21–Sept. 1, Third Army
and left wing of the Fourth Army; 34,000 prisoners,
270 guns.

Battle of the Scarpe, Aug. 26–Sept. 3, First
Army; 16,000 prisoners, 200 guns.

Battle of Havrincourt and Epêhy, Sept. 12–18, Fourth and Third Armies; 12,000 prisoners, 100 guns.

Battle of Cambrai and the Hindenburg Line, Sept. 27–Oct. 5, Fourth, Third and First Armies, which ended in the breaking of the Hindenburg Line and in the capture of 35,000 prisoners and 380 guns.

Battle of Flanders, Sept. 28–Oct. 14, Second Army.

Battle of Le Cateau, Oct. 6–12, Fourth, Third and First Armies.

Battle of the Selle, Oct. 17–25, Fourth and Third Armies, 20,000 prisoners, 475 guns.

Battle of the Sambre, Nov. 1–11, Fourth, Third and First Armies; 19,000 prisoners, 450 guns.'

Foch added :

'Never at any time in history has the British Army achieved greater results in attack than in this un-broken offensive . . . The victory was indeed complete, thanks to the excellence of the Commanders of Armies, Corps and Divisions, thanks above all to the unselfishness, to the wise, loyal and energetic policy of their Commander-in-Chief, who made easy a great combination, and sanctioned a prolonged and gigantic effort.'

In the event, during those last three months of the War, the British Army under Haig captured 188,700 prisoners and 2,840 guns, while all the remaining Allies in the West between them captured 196,700 prisoners and 3,775 guns. It was an amazing and decisive feat.

This I now consider to be the true and only starting point for the study of Haig; but when I wrote the following article in 1961 I took a somewhat different line towards the same conclusions.

HAIG: 1861–1928

The centenary of the birth of Field-Marshal Earl Haig has been marked in a number of ways. The British Legion paid its respects to its founder; the B.B.C. broadcast a typical 'commemorative programme'; Captain Liddel Hart wrote a long article for the *Sunday Times,* and Captain Cyril Falls wrote one in a quite different vein for *The Times* : four books were published attacking Haig's reputation; a series of hostile articles in the *Evening Standard* added their critical voices to the chorus, and that journal steadfastly refused to publish an article putting forward a more friendly view. Controversy about Haig is as sharply defined today as ever. It is important to understand why.

If Haig had been appointed to command the B.E.F. in December 1917, instead of December 1915, and had taken over just in time to weather the storm of the German spring offensive of 1918 and then pass straight into the succession of cumulative victories which produced the Armistice in November, it is unlikely that there would be any argument about him. His place among the 'Great Captains' would scarcely have been contested. He himself, of course, would have considered this proposition to be a 'nonsense'; he would have said that there could not have been a victory in 1918 but for what had gone before in 1916 and 1917,

and that his achievement (or otherwise) is indivisible.
In his final despatch, dated March 21st, 1919, he
wrote :

> '. . . neither the course of the war itself nor the
> military lessons to be drawn therefrom can properly
> be comprehended unless the long succession of
> battles commenced on the Somme in 1916 and
> ended in November of last year on the Sambre are
> viewed as forming part of one great and continuous
> engagement. To direct attention to any single phase
> of that stupendous and incessant struggle, and seek
> in it the explanation of our success to the exclusion
> or neglect of other phases possibly less striking in
> their immediate or obvious consequences, is in my
> opinion to risk the formation of unsound doctrines
> regarding the character and requirements of modern
> war. If the operations of the past $4\frac{1}{2}$ years are re-
> garded as a single continuous campaign, there can
> be recognised in them the same general features and
> the same necessary stages which between forces of
> approximately equal strength have marked all the
> conclusive battles of history.'

It is entirely characteristic that, in asserting his final
victory, he should identify himself completely with all
that had preceded it; and it is precisely what preceded
it that has done most harm to his memory.

The whole matter can be summed up in two words :
Somme and Passchendaele. In the first of these battles,
the British Army lost over 400,000 men in four and
a half months, 57,000 of them on the first day alone;
in the second, it lost 244,000 men in four months.

There was no spectacular disaster at Passchendaele to compare with the first day of the Somme; conditions were much the same in both battles (some survivors of both have firmly stated that Somme conditions, particularly in the Ancre Valley, were the worse of the two); the gains in ground in both were microscopic in relation to the global scope of the War itself. Huge losses, great suffering, small apparent results, profound disappointment, these are the ingredients of the case against Haig. It has been most forcefully expressed, as one might expect, by the late Earl Lloyd George: 'I never met any man in a high position who seemed to me so utterly devoid of imagination.' A less elegant judgement is quoted by the present Earl Lloyd George: ' "Brilliant to the top of his army boots," father said.'

Successive writers have found in this analysis the reasons for the dreadful casualties and the slow progress of the British Army during the first two years of Haig's command-in-chief. Insensitive, unreceptive, obstinate and above all unimaginative—how could such a man be expected to do anything but blunder on from slaughter to slaughter? they would ask. If, of course, it should prove to be the case that he was not any of these things, then one might have to take another look at the slaughter, and many fine theories might go astray; if it should also prove to be the case that no general in any country at that time was able to avoid similar slaughter under certain conditions, while the best achievements of any of them are fully matched by Haig's, then one might find oneself drawn to the more sober conclusion of Sir Winston Churchill that: 'He

might be, surely he was, unequal to the prodigious
scale of events; but no one else was discerned as his
equal or his better.' And this I firmly believe to be the
truth.

Imagination takes many forms. The imagination of
the poet, the imagination of the inventor, the imagination of the statesman, or of the social reformer, to name
but four expressions of this elusive quality, are hard to
balance against each other. But whatever form of expression it may take, the quality itself is usually recog-
nisable when it appears. One can also make a rough
and ready division into imagination on the 'grand'
scale, and that which functions on a more immediate,
lesser scale. It is not difficult, if one is disposed to look,
to find imaginative manifestations in Haig at both
these levels. In my opinion Haig displayed, four times
in his career, imagination at the highest level of all, that
which affects the destiny and policy of the nation, and
I consider four times to be very good going. Matched
with 'lower' scale demonstrations of the same gift, this
forces any serious student to approach his deeds in a
spirit of, at the very least, rational and sympathetic
inquiry. If ill befalls a stupid man, there is no cause for
wonder; but when ill befalls an intelligent and imaginative man, that is something that deserves the most
serious thought. When the same phenomenon is observed throughout the civilised world, one perceives
that one is in the presence of a very large issue indeed.

Let us now examine Haig's four moments of 'grand'
scale imagination. (I say 'moments'; it must not be
supposed that they were fleeting; these were percep-
tions which, once experienced, remained with him as

guiding principles.) The first was in 1906, when Haldane summoned him to the War Office on grounds
which he has clearly stated :

> '. . . after surveying the whole Army, I took it
> upon myself to ask Lord Haig, who was then in
> India, to come over to this country and to think for
> us. From all I could discover even then, he seemed
> to be the most highly equipped thinker in the British
> Army.'

This was at a time when thinkers were needed, for
Haldane was engaged upon the most sweeping con-
structive reform in the British Army's history. Haig's
contribution to the Haldane reforms has been freely
acknowledged though it is generally conveniently forgotten; his collaboration with Haldane, himself one of
the leading intellects of the age in the fields of Politics,
Law and Philosophy, should be indicative. The essence
of what these two men were engaged upon (with a
handful of others likewise gifted) was the creation of
the Citizen Army without which, they saw, Britain
could not even take the field in the war of the future.

It is not being asserted that Haig was the only
soldier who saw the need for a Citizen Army long before the War; outside Haldane's circle there were those
who, like Lord Roberts, campaigned for National
Service. But it was Haig and Haldane together who
made the Citizen Army a practicality. Years before the
War broke out Haig realised that it would be a pro-
tracted struggle, and that the full resources of the
nation would be required to win it. This was a rare
vision; the failure of successive governments to orga-

nise those resources throughout the duration of the War (indeed, one might say until 1941), shows how far in advance of contemporary thinking he was. When the War came it fell upon him, under the worst possible conditions, to transform the citizens into soldiers. The outcome of the battles of 1918 shows that he succeeded in this task; the truest evaluation of 1916 is that which sees in the grim struggles of that year the completion of the first stage in the process. But the beginning was in 1906, the fruit of imagination.

Haig's second important insight was one whose seeds were planted in him as early as the retreat from Mons, and which steadily grew in him until, by June 1915, it was a firm conviction : namely that the French would not be able to go on shouldering the main burden of fighting Germany in the West for long, and that the British would have to take most of that burden off them. No other British leader, civilian or military, grasped this truth as Haig did. Lord Kitchener glimpsed it but recoiled from the consequences; Sir John French missed it; Sir Henry Wilson was blinded by his emotional attitudes towards France; Sir William Robertson approached it, but never with Haig's clarity; the efforts of the most vigorous politicians to divert the main British effort from the Western Front show how far they were from appreciating this underlying reality. With Haig it was a guiding motive.

Not only that, but he also realised that, while shouldering the main burden of battle, the British would still have to submit to the general control of operations by the French—a selfless, broadminded recognition from which he never departed, and which was unique. The collapse of the French Army in 1917 is proof enough that Haig was right; the inner truth of that sombre year is only to be reached through the understanding that during it the British Army was taking over from their exhausted Allies. This has nothing to do with the often-repeated argument that Pétain was continually appealing to Haig to go on with the Passchendaele offensive. Haig's policy was arrived at on broad grounds; Pétain's appeals are a myth. On the contrary, it was Haig who was appealing to Pétain to fulfil his promises to co-operate with the British— and receiving in return little more than polite apologies and more promises. Haig was undeterred; for over two years he had known what the British Army would have to do, and now the hour had come. The tragedy of 1917 is that, through mismanagement at the highest level of war direction, the very considerable advantages won by the Allies in 1916 (freely admitted by the Germans) were thrown away in the following year.

In 1918 Haig became both the architect of victory and the first leader to perceive its imminence. It was Haig's initiative, following an alarming conference with Pétain on March 24th at which the latter had spoken of the possibilities of the British and French Armies being cut off from each other, which led to the appointment of Foch as Generalissimo. Much has been made of this appointment; it proved to have considerable value (nothing less, one feels, could have woven the expanding American effort securely into Allied operations), but it was never more valuable than in its first moments when Foch was enabled to overrule Pétain and prevent a French withdrawal upon Paris.

It was Haig who insisted that Foch's command should extend over the whole Western Front, not merely the sector threatened by the German attack. These two interventions alone would suffice to give him a leading place in the march to victory, but they are not his main achievement in 1918. It was his perception that the War could be ended in that year that counts most. This was based on the conviction which he had formed before the German assault even began, that if it failed (and he was certain that it would) Germany would be ruined. It was just over a week after the magnificent opening of the British counter-attack at Amiens on August 8th, when Foch was planning a decisive blow in April 1919, and Churchill was visiting Haig with thoughts of the campaign of 1920 in mind, that Haig told the latter : '. . . we ought to do our utmost to get a decision this autumn'. On that belief he based all his future actions; his vindication came just under three months later, and with it the ending of the slaughter.

These three large ideas—the need for a Citizen Army, the need for Britain to take over the French burden, and the need to grasp the opportunity of swift victory—indicate the intellectual quality of the man. His human quality, the working of the same insight through the channels of compassion and feeling, are revealed in his developing awareness of the nation's duty towards its Citizen Army when that Army was disbanded, and above all to those who had been maimed in her service, and to the descendants of those who had died. By the middle of 1916 he was becoming aware of the scale of this problem; all through the harassing preoccupations of 1917 it was in his mind.

In February of that year he addressed the Army Council on this subject, in a long and carefully thought-out memorandum. After the Armistice he tried to put pressure on the Government to act for the ex-Servicemen by refusing honours. When all else failed, he gave the remaining years of his life to the formation and guidance of the British Legion which, far more than the statue which stands outside the premises of this Institution, is his true memorial, and an everlasting mockery of the notion that he was 'insensitive' to the sufferings and virtues of the men whom he commanded. The memory, not yet extinct amongst us, of men in uniform begging in the streets during the 1920s indicates once more that Haig was out ahead.

On the lower level of immediate impact, impartial examination reveals Haig in a similar light. This is not to be wondered at; it would have been odd if a man capable of grasping such significant concepts as those listed above had shown no ability to apply the same gift to actual operations. But, of course, that is not so. If one takes the trouble to list the big, effective surprises of the War—such phenomena as, for example, the bewildering scope of the first German onset based on the Schlieffen Plan, or the counterstroke on the Marne, or the introduction of unrestricted submarine warfare —one finds that the balance-sheet on the German and Allied sides is roughly equal. (This reflects well on Germany, since she alone supplied the credit items for the Central Powers.) But if one examines the Allied list, one finds that at least half the occasions in it are British achievements under Haig. Seven important surprises attributable to him can be named without further thought: the novelty of the short bombardment at Neuve Chapelle; the dawn attack on the Somme on July 14th, 1916; the first tank attack on September 15th (no arguments about this, if the first use of gas is to go down on the German list!); the opening attack from the caves of Arras; the Battle of Messines; the first mass tank attack in history at Cambrai; the stunning surprise of August 8th, 1918. This is not a bad beginning; others might be added.

The truth is that so far from being 'inflexible', Haig was immensely (one might almost at times say, naively) interested in new developments, new techniques, new weapons. During his period as a Corps and Army Commander, his diary contains numbers of sketches and diagrams, with full explanations, of innovations which had been brought to his attention. His Corps was the first to develop trench artillery, and the Stokes mortar, which became standard, was first demonstrated in his Army. But nothing is more striking than his attitude towards the tanks.

Every entry in his diary referring to tanks, *even before he had seen them,* long before they had appeared in action, and afterwards when many doubted, is enthusiastic and approving. The most significant of all is the entry of September 18th, three days after what many regarded as the disappointing début of the new arm, when Haig suggested to the Admiral commanding at Dover 'that he should carry out experiments with special flat-bottomed boats for running ashore and landing a line of tanks on the beach . . . The Admiral was delighted with the idea, and is to go to the Admiralty with a view to having special boats made.' This prognostication of the L.S.T.s and L.C.T.s of World War II, and the amphibious operations which they made possible, ought to dispose once and for all of the silly assertion that he lacked originality. The hard facts that, under him, tanks made their first appearance in war; scored their first significant success; and subsequently played an outstanding part in the decisive victory of the War, entitle Haig to be regarded as their 'god-father'. If any non-Tank Corps general has the right to the black beret, it is Haig.

In the entirely novel field of war organisation, also, his role was of lasting importance. It has to be remembered that no administrative apparatus beyond that required for one Army Corps had existed in the British Army in peacetime. In order to staff the headquarters of the Expeditionary Force, the War Office was practically swept clean of experienced Staff Officers. The lack of such officers, at all levels from G.H.Q. to Brigade, was a permanent weakness to which much of the frustration and loss of the War must be attributed. At G.H.Q. itself, and in the higher echelons, it could to some extent be rectified by the recruitment of experts from civilian life, to manage some of those innumerable activities into which the Army found itself plunged when the B.E.F. expanded to the size of a population larger than that administered by any organ of British local government other than Greater London. It need hardly be said that the introduction of these civilians into the military machine met with tremendous resistance. The arrival of Sir Eric Geddes to superintend railway transport set many a dovecot a-flutter and caused Haig a great deal of trouble. But, almost alone among those of his rank, he had no doubts whatever about the necessity for this appointment and other similar ones to do with roads, docks, inland waterways, and a whole range of problems hitherto matched only in civilian life. 'To put soldiers who have no practical experience of these matters in such positions, merely because they are generals and colonels, must result in utter failure', he wrote in his diary. Haig's relations with Geddes, and with every other genuine 'expert' who came his way, are a clear indication of his detachment from the dead atmosphere of traditionalism for its own sake.

Objective inspection, then, shows us an unmistakable picture of a man of long sight and practical ability; in spite of this, he was concerned, throughout the War, in bloody 'slogging matches', many of which, whether large or small in scope, bore the distinct hallmarks of ineptitude. There is a contradiction here which deserves the most careful thought and analysis. Two fundamental factors may be discerned in it : one was a fault of Haig's, the other not. His weakness as a commander, and it recurs time after time, was his reluctance to interfere with his subordinates once he had set them a task. This was partly a matter of loyalty carried to what we may consider an exaggerated pitch, but it was also in part a characteristic weakness of the man of principle, who, having worked out a correct method, is reluctant to depart from it even when, for special reasons, it does not produce results. Examples of the same attitude in civilian life are too abundant in all ages to require mention.

It is a fact, however, that Haig's personal intervention in situations, to the point of overruling the man on the spot, was all too often much later than it should have been. Whenever he did intervene it was always on the side of reason and common sense; but not until after the disaster following the initial success of Cambrai did he make it a regular habit to do this. In 1918, certainly from the beginning of the last great offensive, he spent almost the whole of his time in his Advanced Headquarters, with only a handful of Staff Officers, living in a train, so as to be beside each one of his Army Commanders at moments of decision. The result of the campaign speaks for itself.

The second factor has nothing to do with Haig. Partly, it is to do with Britain's total lack of experience of continental war on the modern scale, with the huge difference between what happened in 1914-1918 and what had always happened in the 'little' wars conducted by a small Regular Army in the past. It is to do with the national smugness and selfishness which had always accepted that the security of the nation could be left to a small band of professionals in the Navy and Army. World war in the twentieth century made short work of such beliefs, but a country which had recoiled from the contemplation of its responsibilities, recoiled no less from the cost of them when this was brought home to her. The continental Powers (including America) were better prepared for the psychological shock of their dreadful losses; they were not so well prepared as to be able to avoid these losses. The final statement about Haig must be that where he failed, he failed in the same manner and in the company of such names as these: Joffre, Foch, Nivelle,

Pétain, Moltke, Falkenhayn, Ludendorff, Conrad, Cadorna, a sequence of Russian leaders, Sir John French, Sir Ian Hamilton and General Pershing. Where he succeeded, he did so on account of superior endowments to those of any of the distinguished officers named above. Where he was defeated, it was by 'the prodigious scale of events'; where he won, it was by professional merit. It was left to his enemies to call him 'Master of the Field'.

Many distinguished officers served under Haig, whose names are hardly known today; they have been obliterated by the impersonality of the Western Front, in which their soldiers were also swallowed up. Allenby is remembered, because of his Palestine successes; Rawlinson may mean something, because of his battles on the Somme; Gough became identified with the disaster which befell his Fifth Army in March 1918. Some people—not many—remember Plumer; he was, in some ways, the most talented of them all. When Lloyd George was looking for a possible successor to Haig in 1918, Plumer's name was immediately canvassed. He let it be known that he did not wish to supplant his chief. Yet, even before Haig became C.-in-C., when Sir John French was about to depart, according to one divisional commander: 'Popular opinion pointed to Haig as the prétendant, though Plumer would probably have had the army's vote.' This was long before he had won his important victories. There were reasons for this confidence in him.

A SOLDIER'S SOLDIER

If one could imagine oneself wandering down some long portrait gallery of Britain's military leaders, looking for the original model and inspiration of David Low's Colonel Blimp, one would consider one's quest ended at the picture of Herbert Charles Onslow Plumer, Field-Marshal the Viscount Plumer of Messines, G.C.B., G.C.M.G. One of the most famous war correspondents of his day wrote of him: 'In appearance he was almost a caricature of an old-time British general, with his ruddy, pippin-cheeked face, with white hair and a fierce little white moustache, and blue, watery eyes, and a little pot-belly and short legs.' 'Daddy' Plumer: the most consistently reliable and successful British Army Commander of the First World War: a very great soldier, whose title stems from an outstanding feat of arms: now an almost unknown name.

Herbert Plumer was born in 1857, and his great victory at Messines was won in 1917. Conceived and carried out as a limited operation, lasting only three days, it was beyond question one of the most brilliant successes of the whole War on the British sector of the Western Front. It was also, in a sense, prophetic. A German observer of the opening of the battle, at 3.10 a.m. on June 4th, 1917, after half an hour's calm during which nightingales could be heard singing in

distant woods, described it in these words: '. . . nineteen gigantic roses with carmine petals, or . . . enormous mushrooms . . . rose up slowly and majestically
out of the ground and then split into pieces with a
mighty roar, sending up multicoloured columns of
flame mixed with a mass of earth and splinters high
into the sky'. These mushroom explosions of 1917 were
the effects of nineteen huge mines, planted at intervals
along the Messines-Wytschaete Ridge, containing
957,000 lb. of explosive, all detonated together. The
shock was felt distinctly in London; on the spot it was
like an earthquake. And before its reverberations could
die away, they were caught up and redoubled in the
fury of a barrage of 2,330 guns and howitzers. Behind
this, 80,000 infantry rose from their lines to assault the
ridge. When they had captured their objectives, their
losses were one-fifth of the anticipated total—a unique
event in the history of that war. Such was Plumer's
masterpiece.

What sort of a man was he? How did he do it? The
secret lies in a comment that *The Spectator* made on
him in 1904, when he became a member of the Army
Council: 'General Plumer is emphatically the
"soldier's soldier". One of the half-dozen living generals whom the whole Army unites in praising.' The
reason why this Regular Army officer won such acclaim
was that he was able to break the shackles of convention that bound almost all his contemporaries. And the
reason for that is to be found in the nature of his early
service, which all took place in Africa.

His first major assignment was to clear up the mess
after the Jameson raid, and almost immediately after-

wards he commanded the British forces in the Mata-
bele War, working in close liaison with Cecil Rhodes,
until the campaign ended with Rhodes's famous
Indaba in the Matoppo Hills. When the South African
War broke out, Plumer's detachment maintained a
precarious but continuous link with Baden-Powell in
Mafeking and eventually he relieved the place, using
much the same techniques of deception and ruse as
Baden-Powell did in the defence. He then went on to
become one of the most conspicuously successful
column-commanders against the elusive Boer leaders,
De Wet, Hertzog, Brand and Fourie. Throughout this
period his forces consisted mainly of 'colonials'—
Rhodesians and other African contingents, and men
from the Dominions of Canada, Australia, New
Zealand. With these hard-bitten, individualistic, unorthodox troops, formal methods would have been
disastrous. From his contact with them, Plumer
learned an unforgettable lesson about the human rela-
tionships of war : he learned that the confidence of
every individual in the ranks is the first objective that a
leader must capture. Also, from all this, he acquired
an unusually extensive experience of independent command, with all the responsibility of decision that it
implies.

When it came to applying these lessons in the search-
ing tests of 1914-1918, Plumer reduced them to three
elements. He was appointed to command the unfortunate Second Army in the Ypres Salient in May 1915,
as it reeled back from the horrors of the first gas attack.
His Chief of Staff from June 1916 onwards was Sir
Charles Harington, an exceptionally talented Staff

Officer, and, significantly, fresh from a staff appointment in the Canadian Corps. The two men got on together from the first, and forged one of these military partnerships, like Foch-Weygand, Napoleon-Berthier, Hindenburg-Ludendorff, which are always so fruitful. Harington defined Plumer's 'elements of success' as three T's—Trust, Training and Thoroughness.

Of these, the most significant was Trust, for other officers could also be thorough, and others could train men. But Plumer's kind of Trust was uncommon. He began with his staff. At the daily Army Commander's Conference every department was shown the whole picture, everyone knew what everyone else was doing, everyone tried to help everyone else. Inter-departmental jealousy did not exist in the Second Army. Then came the next point. As Harington says : 'We were Plumer's team. We were privileged to know his mind and his wishes and it was our job to carry his spirit of trust and helpfulness to the lower formations in the Army . . . It was our business to be out helping others with their difficulties.' This was a novel concept of staff duties in those days.

But Plumer's object was to extend his 'network of trust' throughout the whole Army—and how he succeeded is related by Sir Philip Gibbs, then a war correspondent and no lover of war or generals. 'There was a thoroughness of method, a minute attention to detail, a care for the comfort and spirit of the men, throughout the Second Army Staff which did at least inspire the troops with the belief that whatever they did in the fighting lines had been prepared, and would be supported, with every possible help that organisation could provide.'

So much for Trust. In this respect the Second Army established a reputation which contrasted sharply with some others, and excelled all. Training is a more limited matter, each historical context requiring its own special approach. For us the lesson to be drawn from Plumer's methods is again the stress that he placed upon the regimental officer, whether the battalion commanders, whom he drew in by batches to Army headquarters to broaden their picture of events, or the junior officers, on whom he saw that the tactical onus must increasingly fall. Plumer's training was fundamentally a training of individuals and small units : and this was the direction in which the future lay.

The thoroughness of the Second Army under Plumer and Harington was a byword. One has only to reflect that some of the mines that exploded at Messines on June 4th, 1917, were begun in December 1915; that some of the mine galleries stretched nearly half a mile to bring them under the enemy's position; that the whole mining operation in this wet area, with its danger from gas and flood and enemy countermining, with all the problems of spoil disposal, was of a complexity beyond words, to see the case. To take one point only : for the deep mines at Messines, a layer of blue clay ('London clay') had to be passed through. Any sign of blue clay on the surface would have given the game away; so every scrap of spoil had to be carried off to a great distance, or reburied. So successfully was this done, that only in April did the Germans obtain a hint of what was going on, and a few weeks later they knew only too well.

But although the mines supplied the melodrama of Messines, it was his handling of artillery that was the chief factor in Plumer's victories. He understood very clearly how much this arm dominated the modern battlefield. For Messines his artillery concentration, at one piece for every seven yards of front, was the highest yet reached in the British Army. But he was to do better still. For Messines, although it gave him his title, and was the most complete integral victory of the War, was not his greatest test. Three months later, when the first phase of the battle known to history as Third Ypres, and to the man in the street as Passchendaele, had sunk into slimy disaster under the direction of the Fifth Army, Plumer was called on to take the leading part. During the five weeks of September and early October, wielding an instrument of some thirty divisions, three-quarters of a million men, a far vaster army than any other British commander has ever had under his immediate hand, Plumer struck three huge blows at the Germans, one by one, and in each the artillery achieved an efficiency and effect unparalleled in our annals.

The three sub-battles of the Menin Road Ridge (September 20th), Polygon Wood (September 26th) and Broodseinde (October 4th) almost brought the German Army to its knees. In each case, an unmistakable success was achieved, with large numbers of prisoners and, in the last case, according to the Official History, 'the number of dead Germans seen on the battlefield exceeded that observed in any previous

British assault of the War'. Well it might, for, if we take the first of these as a pattern, we find the British artillery playing an unprecedented part. For the Menin Road Battle the guns and howitzers numbered nearly 1,000 on a 4,000-yard front. Over 200 of them were devoted to counter-battery work. The rest made up the protective barrage, *1,000 yards deep,* in five belts of five, one of which was provided by 240 machine-guns. Never had British infantry gone into action with such support. The result of this battle and the two that followed it, under Plumer and his indefatigable staff, was devastating. And though the campaign itself petered out in rain and mud and misery, the last word on Plumer's achievement is the Australian Official Historian's question : 'Let the student, looking at the prospect as it appeared at noon on 4th October, ask himself : "In view of three step-by-step blows, all successful, what will be the result of three more in the next fortnight?" ' For the day of the great Australian victory at Broodseinde was the day that the German historians call 'the black day', admitting that the German Army was only saved after it by rain. Plumer calls it 'the best thing done by the Second Army'. We may add, 'the best thing done by Plumer'. But who, outside Australia, ever hears of Broodseinde today?

And so it emerges that the little old white-haired, pot-bellied gentleman with his pince-nez, whose appearance seems to epitomise every fault in the British military character, was, in fact, one of the most modern soldiers of his generation. If all that has been said above reads as *vieux jeu,* as unsurprising normal procedure, it is because many of Plumer's methods became the standard procedure of the Second World War. The warfare of our age became more and more mechanical, and more and more complex in its reliance upon the machinery of production and engines of destruction. Without organisation at the highest level, all this complexity becomes unmanageable and chaotic. Plumer's sense of organisation was therefore a cardinal principle, a *sine qua non* of modern war. But where he added the special touch of insight was in his realisation that the mechanical impersonality of war requires to be counteracted by the greatest moral stimulus. The soldier may be a pawn, but he must never feel it. Only Plumer, in that war, was able to reach down to the spirit of the lonely, frightened man in the forward sap, and lift it up a little from the mire. As Harington says: 'He had been a regimental soldier, and he never forgot it.'

Because organisation was so important, and because Harington was an organiser of supreme quality, some writers have held that Harington, in fact, was the genius of the Second Army. So perhaps Harington should have the last word on Plumer: 'His own personality so permeated the whole army that our task was made easy.' And finally: 'I say at once that he was the supreme head, he listened to all, and then made his decision which was final.' It is a pity that we forget such men so easily.

The question continues to be asked: was the blood-bath on the Western Front inevitable? Was there no other way? My own view will have become apparent by now: that there was not. Yet there remains an evident and disturbing contrast between generalship on the Western Front between 1914 and 1918, and the performances of the 'great captains' of history. I believe that this is largely an unreal comparison, but it continues to exert a fascination, and such is the power of myth that this fascination, over many years, has chiefly sprung from the exploits of Napoleon.

Big Battalions

THE NAPOLEONIC LEGACY

In October 1914 Mr. Lloyd George, who was then Chancellor of the Exchequer, was visiting the Western Front. The so-called 'Race to the Sea' was over; the encounter battles which had marked the climax of the simultaneous attempts of both sides to outflank the opposing line had ended in deadlock; in the First Battle of Ypres, and in the innumerable forgotten, but desperate, grapples along the front from Flanders to Switzerland, the structure of the War as it was largely to remain for over four years was being moulded. Already the symptoms of persistent deadlock were visible. Lloyd George was calling upon General de Castelnau, commander of the French Second Army, an officer with a very high reputation for strategic ability who was later to rise to positions of special eminence at the General Headquarters of the French Army. Lloyd George wrote :

'His personality created a deep impression on our minds. He was a short man with a high forehead and intelligent dark eyes—quiet and grave in demeanour. . . . I asked how many men were under his command, and he said there were nine corps. "Well," I remarked, "that is a greater army than

Napoleon ever commanded in any single battle."
His answer was a kind of soliloquy. "Ah, Napoleon,
Napoleon. If he were here now, he'd have thought
of the 'something else'." '

This remark had a profound effect upon Lloyd
George which time did not diminish. Writing of a
much later stage of the War, he said :

> 'It had become a war of endurance. The strategy
> on both sides was unimaginative and commonplace.
> There was no military genius on either side to devise,
> execute and exploit a stroke that transformed the
> course of the War and determined the result.
> Castelnau's penetrating observation about Napo-
> leon still held good. "Had he been here he would
> have thought of the something else." No General
> had yet discovered it.'

This criticisim of the generalship displayed during the
First World War won wide acceptance, and with it the
implied comparison with the achievements of the
'Great Captains'—Napoleon in particular, since his
influence on modern war was visibly more direct than
that of Frederick the Great, Marlborough or Turenne,
to take three other recent examples, and apparently
very much more immediate than that of classical
heroes such as Hannibal, or Alexander the Great.

Castelnau's saying, as well as setting the tone of
many subsequent critiques, reflected a frame of mind
that was not only widespread, but almost obligatory in
the French Army at the time. The worship of Napoleon, industriously fostered by his supporters and

numerous relatives from the very outset of his second exile, had by 1914 become an intrinsic part of the French Army's revival after the débâcle of 1870, despite the fact that that collapse occurred under another Bonaparte. It is instructive to examine Castelnau's expression of what had already become a widely held idea; the question arises : was there any truth in it ? The answer to that question may expose Napoleon himself in a light which, if not new, is certainly less familiar than the adulation that he continues to receive not only in France but elsewhere. It may also prompt second thoughts about the men who have been so unfavourably compared with him—and about those who are responsible for the comparisons.

Two factors swiftly assert themselves as we consider our question : first, Napoleon's actual performance, and, secondly, the assessment and interpretation of it by later generations of students at Staff Colleges and elsewhere. One cannot separate these factors too adamantly, because it is precisely their inter-relation that ultimately concerns us. One has, therefore, to be constantly casting an eye forward, when considering what Napoleon did, at what was made of it later. This 'double vision' instantly suggests that there was a curious illogicality at the root of all those studies of Napoleon which concentrated upon his prowess and status as a 'Great Captain'. The basic, final truth about Napoleon, after all, is that *he failed*; as Captain Liddell Hart has written : 'it is well to remember that St. Helena became his destination'.

Now this is a truth that generation after generation of worshippers has glossed over, starting with the parti-

sans who began work on the Napoleonic legend while
he was still on St. Helena, with the specific object of
getting him off it. As one reads the glowing recitals of
the Emperor's conquests and glories; as one meets
their innumerable memorials in the monuments and
place-names of Paris and every other French city to
this day, one is almost persuaded that St. Helena has
nothing to do with the case, that Napoleon's arrival
there was a sort of accident, or at the very least, that it
was something that 'ought not' to have happened, a
strange reversal of true form. One is vividly reminded
of the reports which one reads in certain papers every
time England loses the Ashes, or some other inter-
national sporting event. Every reason is put forward
except the true one, which is simply that the other
side played better, that our own side was actually bad.
And this is the truth about Napoleon; St. Helena
always *was* his destination. The fact was disguised for
many years by the ineptitude of his enemies, the
monarchs and generals of the crumbling Ancien Ré-
gime. Afterwards, it was deliberately concealed by
propaganda.

Once this truth is seen, much else falls into place. It
is not, after all, surprising, if studies which ought to be
studies of failure but instead are treated as studies of
success bring confusion and further failure in their
train. And this is precisely what happened. Nor is it
simply a matter of Napoleon being defeated *in the
end*; he was frequently defeated all through his career
and mostly by the play of the very elements which
brought about his final fall.

His campaign in Italy in 1796 has been the object

of endless inspections and analysis. This is not without reason; it was, beyond doubt, a brilliant affair, a remarkable instance of precision in the working out of military action. At bottom, what it reveals is the great advantage of an active general, with an active policy, over inert generals with scarcely any policy at all except to hope for the best. Even so, it was a fine piece of work. But what followed? The sequel was the expedition to Egypt in 1798. And what is one to make of that? The answer is that already, before he was even First Consul, let alone Emperor, Napoleon revealed the grip of a maniacal power-complex which robbed him of reason and balance. The Egyptian Expeditionary Force was the first French Army that he lost and abandoned; it was by no means the last. But the central fact here is that under almost any other conditions than those prevailing in Revolutionary France, Napoleon would surely have been disgraced for this episode, perhaps shot, but at any rate considered unfit for further employment. There would then have been no Empire, no legend and possibly much less suffering and loss of life in Europe.

Instead of being court-martialled and punished, Napoleon was able to so exploit the disturbed political condition of France as to procure his own advancement successively to the heights of First Consul and of Emperor. '*L'état c'est moi*' became a statement more profoundly true of his position than it ever was of Louis XIV's because his person was far more closely identified with military success, while the civil affairs of the state were conducted by machinery vastly more modern and efficient than any possessed by 'Le Roi Soleil'.

The huge energy of the man permeated everything; its particular outlet was war; its sanction was victory. A remarkable string of victories ensued: Marengo (1800), Ulm (1805), Austerlitz (1805), Jéna (1806), Friedland (1807), Wagram (1809) and lesser occasions without number. Austria, Russia and Prussia, two great Empires and a rising state with an already established military reputation of the highest order, were convincingly beaten in battle, whether they fought together or alone. This was the stuff that legends are made of, and it is small wonder that the legends grew. They were, of course, carefully fostered by Napoleon himself. 'Moral force more so than numbers decides victory,' Napoleon later pronounced, in the course of delivering the strange series of aphorisms and wise saws which so often seem utterly unrelated to his own destiny. The notions of French invincibility and of his own genius were part of the moral force which he wielded. Against coalitions, against second-rate generals, against the mixed and inefficient armies of the European Powers, it was terribly effective. When these three factors were subtracted, the story was different.

On this analysis, it is possible to discover the turning-point in the tide of Napoleonic triumph in the month of June 1808. The British Government had decided to support the insurrection of the Spanish and Portuguese peoples against French invasion with an expeditionary force. A thirty-nine-year-old Lieutenant-General with an Indian reputation, Sir Arthur Wellesley, was appointed to command the force. At a dinner party shortly before he sailed, one of his guests noticed that he seemed silent and preoccupied, and ventured to ask the reason for this. Wellesley replied :

'Why, to say the truth, I am thinking of the French that I am going to fight. I have not seen them since the campaign in Flanders, when they were capital soldiers, and a dozen years of victory under Buonaparte, must have made them better still. They have besides, it seems, a new system of strategy which has out-manœuvred and overwhelmed all the armies of Europe. 'Tis enough to make one thoughtful; but no matter; my die is cast, they may overwhelm me, but I don't think they will outmanœuvre me. First, because I am not afraid of them, as everybody else seems to be; and secondly, because if what I hear of their system of manœuvres be true, I think it is a false one as against steady troops. I suspect all the continental armies were more than half beaten before the battle was begun. I, at least, will not be frightened beforehand.'

Here, at last, was a general who was not susceptible to the moral force; there remained only the 'system of manœuvres'—and according to Wellesley, this was a false one. It was neither conceit nor necromancy that prompted him to this view : it was a sound professional judgement on existing evidence.

Two considerations tend to be ignored when the resonant roll of Napoleon's victories is called : first, that it can be matched with an equally striking roll call of defeats; secondly, the nature of the victories themselves. The run of spectacular success really ended with the overthrow of Prussia after Jéna—that is to say, as early as 1806. The next great battle which Napoleon fought, the precursor of his success at Friedland, was Eylau, a grim and bloody struggle in a snowstorm against the stubborn soldiery of Russia. Eylau was a drawn battle but in effect a defeat for Napoleon. In just the same way, Wagram was preceded by Aspern-Essling, very nearly a disaster for the French. If Borodino was a French victory, then the meaning of the word is transformed. There was nothing of victory in the 1812 campaign. There were delusive flashes in 1813—Bautzen and Dresden; they ended in the catastrophe of Leipzig. The 1814 campaign was full of brilliance and glitter; it closed in abdication. In 1815, only two days separated the deceitful promise of Ligny from the final ruin of Waterloo.

The truth is that, all through these years of apparent Imperial splendour, Napoleon himself was suffering defeats in the field which it required all his address to retrieve, and which were, in fact, bleeding to death the nation behind him. Meanwhile, in the Peninsula, it was being demonstrated by Wellington that there was nothing in French methods or French capacity that could not be dealt with, in Napoleon's absence. Even in his presence there were severe flaws in both, the study of which would have been more rewarding to military students than that of his conquests.

If we seek to penetrate the essence of the Napoleonic method, we find that it consisted in a remarkable synthesis of mass and movement. The mass was put at his disposal by the unleashing of French national energy brought about by the Revolution—in other words, by

conscription. The movement ensued from the untram-
melling of his own energy, when he assumed supreme
and dictatorial power over the state. This enabled him
to move directly and immediately against his targets at
a rate that bewildered and demoralised the forces of
old-fashioned monarchies and coalitions. The dazzling
results which ensued have obscured the true nature of
Napoleonic battles, and the special circumstances in
which alone his prior manœuvres could bear fruit. His
own axioms have added to the obscurity.

Thus, in after years, generations of students exalted
into a sacred dogma his dictum that armies should
'march divided, and fight united'. This is to miss the
central point that armies which march divided run the
constant risk of fighting divided, too. But circumstances
may compel them to march divided; Napoleon's worshippers have translated his recognition and acceptance
of this compulsion into an oracle. At the root of military movement is the question of supply. The French
armies of the period supplied themselves by 'living off
the country'. There were few parts of Europe in those
days which could continously support large bodies of
soldiers in this way. Consequently, Napoleon *had* to
march divided, or give up all idea of speed; the reasonably well-developed road systems of France,
northern Italy, Austria and central Germany enabled
him to do this. Outside them, in Spain, where 'small
armies are defeated and large armies starve', or in
Russia, he floundered and was lost.

Yet, even in the moments of his success, on the
ground that favoured him, we may observe in Napoleon's battles the dangers imposed by his system of

movement and the absence of any tactical system capable of compensating this. Time after time, we find him in the posture of waiting for someone to turn up. At Marengo, it was Desaix who arrived in the nick of time; Austerlitz was made possible by Bernadotte's arrival; at Jéna, two detached corps failed to come up at all—Bernadotte's and Davoust's; the latter, by all the rules of war, should have been cut to pieces, but instead won a brilliant independent victory at Auerstadt which the Emperor calmly appropriated to himself; Eylau would have been a disaster but for Ney's appearance; Wagram was preceded by a frantic search for troops; Ligny and Quatre Bras were indecisive because D'Erlon's corps marched all day to and fro between the battles, taking part in neither; at Waterloo, Napoleon's eye was glued upon a horizon over which Grouchy never appeared.

These were the risks of 'marching divided'; against good generals, they would have been fatal. But what else could Napoleon do, if he desired to make his mass effective? And it was the mass that he depended on; for when battle was joined, his tactical instrument was the bludgeon. One of the outstanding features of all his combats was their bloodiness; because once in his career (at Ulm) he was able to bring a much smaller army to quick capitulation, a legend was born out of a soldiers' saying : 'The Emperor uses our legs instead of our bayonets.' *It never happened again.* Battle after battle shows us the French soldiers in desperate and decimating conflict, until support arrived; then there would be the 'decisive stroke at the decisive point', massed artillery blasting a hole in the defence, massed heavy cavalry or deep columns of infantry bursting into it, and (in theory) massed light cavalry sweeping the débris from the field. After that, it only remained to count the cost, the thirty or forty per cent or more of casualties that Napoleon was prepared to accept to gain his ends. One searches in vain for subtlety; the only innovation was the extremity of violence; as the quality of the army declined with the merciless destruction of the veterans, the cost of winning became ever higher. Napoleon was, indeed, drawing the picture of modern war; but it passes understanding why he should have been so copiously congratulated for doing so.

How did this affect later generations? The French Revolution had brought the masses back into war; Napoleon had wielded them with the ruthlessness which alone could make them effective; the Industrial Revolution provided means of multiplying them. During the hundred years that followed Waterloo, it is not difficult to see an inevitable progression from the last forlorn onset of the solid battalions of the Imperial Guard up the slopes of Mont St. Jean, to the vain endeavours of their descendants in the French offensive of Artois and Champagne, or the slaughter of the British volunteers at Loos.

On this interpretation, General de Castelnau's remark to Lloyd George becomes entirely meaningless : the fact was that during the central period of the First World War, the generals of both sides were expiating their undigested banquets of Napoleonic propaganda and misleading doctrine—at the expense of their soldiers. If the French theorists led the way towards this wrong appraisal, it is not altogether to be wondered at; the national dream of glory became an obsession after the humiliations of the Franco-Prussian War. The quest for a formula of victory was carried out in an atmosphere of hysteria which ill befits the study of history or any other science.

The solid, objective truth is that, during the intervening hundred years, the character both of movement and of battle had been significantly transformed. The world entered the railway age, which enabled masses beyond Napoleon's dreams to be mobilised and shifted. The steam engine—both the railway locomotive and the steamship—added new dimensions to war. After all the initial blunders of the Crimea, there remains the story of a remarkable long-distance achievement in supply and transportation. The Civil War in the United States had, throughout, the characteristics of a railway war. The devastating Prussian deployment which ruined France in 1870 was made possible by a fuller understanding and use of railways. In Kitchener's Nile campaign, each mile of track completed represented a Dervish defeat. In South Africa, the first glimpse of hope for the British was Roberts's attempt to shake free from the metals; but they defeated the British in the end: the mountainous requirements of a regular army could not be carried by any other means over such terrain.

And so we arrive at 1914, and the spectacle of hosts of literally millions moving against each other, almost entirely by train. Strategy, it has been said, is decided by railway time-tables. This is not altogether true; but it is true enough. There was a bare possibility, in the

early stages—the period of the great sweep of the
German right wing *on foot* through Belgium and
northern France—of reaching a decision before the
marshalling yards, the rolling stock and the time-tables
could impose their inexorable pattern. This possibility
vanished when the masses met, and the Industrial
Revolution's second contribution to the art of battle
was disclosed.

During the nineteenth century, the mechanisation
of war, as of peace, proceded at an unprecedented
pace. This first became visible in the Crimea where, as
operations concentrated around a siege, artillery
played an increasingly dominant role. In America this
development continued as part of a general improvement of firearms which ended by giving the very landscape of war a new appearance. Photographs of, for
example, the Union Army in its positions against
Petersburg are to all intents and purposes pictures of
the First World War. In 1870, despite their weakness
in numbers and hesitant manœuvres, the French might
have maintained themselves far better than they did,
had they shown the remotest understanding of how to
deal with the dominating Prussian artillery—that is, by
adopting the American method of going underground.
But their 'Napoleonic' dignity prevented this; it was
not a thing that Napoleon had ever done, and it did
not occur to the French generals to try it.

On the other hand, the Prussians exposed themselves to the frustration of many promising movements by their inability to grasp the implications of
attack against infantry possessing such a fine modern
weapon as the French Chassepot rifle. Courage and

numbers enabled them to overcome tactical ineptitudes which were a direct product of Napoleonic teaching. And so, all through the century, we have the spectacle of one mechanical device making possible the deployment of larger armies than ever before, while progress along other technical courses makes inevitable the nullification of their efforts.

By November 1914 a complete impasse had been reached. Within weeks the vast armies of the main contestants had settled into the trench positions that they were to hold, with only small changes, until the end. Nothing could break the stalemate, except another break-through in technology — a break-through which, fortunately, had already occurred and now awaited application. This was, quite simply, the internal combustion engine which, in the form of a lorry, offered independence of the railways; in the form of a tank, supplied the answer to the joint problem of barbed wire, machine-guns and artillery; and in the form of the aeroplane added a new dimension to war itself, a new meaning to its national character. Not all of these effects were properly seen in 1918; but enough of them were by then apparent to bring the bloodbath to an end. Meanwhile the loss of life had been frightful, and the very structure of human society in what was known as the 'civilised world' had been shaken to its foundations.

The legacy inherited from Napoleon had proved terrible indeed; attempts to emulate his performance, to follow his 'instructions', had had the almost universal effect of increasing the damage. Generals were encouraged to suppose that there was a 'something else', some flash of genius or element of the supernatural that would provide a way through the deadlock, a masterstroke, if they could only find it. Politicians were hopeful that the generals would display such talents, so that the ultimate cost of policies might not be fully exacted. It was a dream; there was no other way. Only if generals and politicians alike had accepted this could the world have been spared the disaster that fell upon it. It was the ghost of Napoleon, more than any other factor, that blocked this acceptance.

Napoleonic studies reached their fullest intensity in the period following the Franco-Prussian War. It was natural that the country most concerned should be France, preoccupied with the reversal of the decision of 1870-1871. The sense of the *need* for a new Napoleon forced the French General Staff, as it were, to invent one. Germany was less directly affected, since she had her own pundit—Clausewitz; but Clausewitz also was a student of Napoleon.

In France the new study, at first reasonably objective and academic, very soon concentrated upon particular and alluring elements of what was taken to be the Napoleonic method; these were enshrined in sayings, mostly delivered at St. Helena, which are sound enough in themselves, but actually constitute critical commentaries upon his own performances. If it was noticed that some of them are contradictory, this unwelcome fact was not advertised. Above all, in the light of what had befallen the armies of Napoleon III under the hammer-blows of the Prussian onset in 1870, French theorists were drawn into exaggerated belief in the powers of the offensive. Such maxims as :

'It is a very great mistake to allow oneself to be attacked' seemed to supply reason enough for the recent French débâcle. From this it followed that: '. . . one should always be the first to attack'; and from this it was a short step to : 'Once one has decided to invade a country, one must not be afraid to deliver battle, and should seek out the enemy everywhere to fight him.' As to the battle itself : 'The first principle of war is that one should only engage in battle when all troops can be united on the battlefield,' or, put another way : 'The army must be assembled and the greatest force possible concentrated on the battlefield.' And so it was made to appear that the whole business of war boiled down to two things : attacking the enemy immediately, and attacking him in full strength. Napoleon himself, of course, knew better; but he had the advantage of not having to graduate in Napoleonic studies. So, when it suited him, which was very often indeed, he was able to draw upon another maxim altogether : 'The whole art of war consists in a well reasoned and circumspect defensive, followed by rapid and audacious attack.' But this was too much of a contradiction for the students; they preferred to forget that he ever said it. Yet it was one of Napoleon's more penetrating observations; it offers, for example, the key to Wellington's *unbroken* course of victory.

The dangers of such sayings as these to the minds of unfledged and over-wrought pupils can be imagined. As one might confidently suppose, to the dangers of misinterpretation of cryptic oracles, there was added the slavish imitation of particular procedures. A striking example of this was reported by Colonel Reping-

ton, *The Times* Military Correspondent during the
pre-war years and for the first part of the War itself.
He describes how, in a conversation with the French
Military Attaché in 1906, he learned that the French
Army was planning to manœuvre according to a system which Napoleon had used in the Jéna campaign,
exactly one hundred years earlier :

'Major Huguet next explained to me, to my
amazement, that the French plan of concentration
was an adaptation of the Napoleonic lozenge; an
"armée d'avant-garde" of the 6th, 7th and 20th
Army Corps, and the rest of the armies on a front of
forty kilometres, echeloned in depth, with reserve
divisions in third line. I could not stand this at all,
protested vehemently, and pointed out that the
German tactics of envelopment would destroy the
lozenge speedily; that the French would be unable
to use their arms, and that I saw no more certain
means of ruining their army. Subsequently I elabo-
rated my objections in detail at Major Huguet's
request, and fortunately this terribly dangerous plan
was given up, to my great relief. It alarmed me
more than anything else at this time, and made me
suspicious of the French strategists and tacticians.'

Unfortunately, if the French gave up this particular
piece of folly, they adhered to others. The crudity of
their notorious Plan XVII in 1914 requires no adum-
bration; it consisted in no more than a united rush
across the frontier—the offensive spirit gone mad;
the attempt to put even part of it into effect produced
the series of catastrophes for France which are known

as the Battles of the Frontiers; these, in turn, shackled French strategy for the remainder of the War.

Germany, as we have said, was less affected by the Napoleonic myth, but not unaffected. If there was less reason than in France to indulge in worship, nevertheless there were elements in Napoleon's warfare that made a strong appeal to German thinkers. The doctrine of the value of the mass was particularly acceptable to a nation which sought safety and expansion through the steady enlargement of its military forces. The problems of bringing its masses on to the battlefield obsessed the German General Staff; they ignored to a dangerous extent the question of what would happen then. Following their dream of a super-Cannae, they were to find practical obstacles as disconcerting as the French; their answers were all too similar.

The British, on the other hand, with a tradition that ran in every respect counter to that of Napoleon, might at least have been expected to exercise a mitigating effect on the excesses that were committed in his name. Their failure to do this before the War began made it impossible for them to do so effectively when its nature emerged; by then they were caught up irretrievably in the ill fortune which had attended their Allies. It was a sad omission; for Britain alone possessed the practical knowledge and the empirical instinct which might have averted some of the worst calamities. As it was, when her small trained army was expended, Britain could only make the attempt to turn herself into a continental military power, flinging her masses into the cauldron along with the rest. What she did, however, contribute, was the weapon which in the end lifted them out of it, and ensured that the stultifying experiences of that war would not be repeated in the next—the tank. But until this appeared, in sufficient force to be effective, every battle was in truth a Napoleonic battle, a grim, ferocious struggle, settled one way or the other (if at all) by the Napoleonic expedients of more guns, more men, more violence. The trouble was not that the world needed another Napoleon; it was that the spirit of the first Napoleon was still there.

Shortly after the foregoing article appeared (in June 1962), Mr. Brian Bond, of the Department of History of Liverpool University, himself an authoritative historian of the late Victorian and early twentieth-century Army, queried whether I had not 'pushed the argument too far', and whether the tank had not, in fact, provided an answer to the Western Front impasse by the end of 1916. He wrote:

'Unfortunately, the few soldiers who did have the genius to appreciate the full potential of this new instrument of war, combining mobility and firepower, were not among the senior generals. Respect for the hierarchy of command, entailing at the top a group of ageing generals not readily responsive to new ideas and methods, must also be held responsible as well as the myth of Napoleon.'

This is a belief which dies hard; but die it must. I replied:

'Tanks had certainly not appeared "in sufficient force to be effective" by 1916. In conjunction with other factors, they greatly helped to finish the War in 1918, but not until 1940 was their full potential seen. Between 1916-1918 they suffered from two serious defects (more damaging than the errors of generals, "ageing" or otherwise); these were quantity and quality.

'Work began on tanks in March 1915; the first

trial was held in February 1916; in April 1916 (three months *before* the opening of the Battle of the Somme), without seeing them, Lord Haig was counting on achieving "decisive results" from the use of 150 of them; in September 1916 (nearly three months *after* the opening of the battle), only 49 were available. For Arras (April 1917—seven months later and fourteen months after the first trial), 60 were available, many of them repaired Somme veterans. For Cambrai, two years and eight months after their inception, 478 existed. At Amiens, their greatest victory, nine months after Cambrai, there were 534. Yet Haig had asked for 1,000 in September 1916, despite the equivocal character of their first performance. Evidently, design and production difficulties played as great a part in their story as lack of understanding by generals.

'Moreover, useful as the 1916-1918 tanks were for breaking into enemy positions and saving infantry lives, they were not weapons of exploitation such as we saw in World War II. Their "mobility" over rough ground was often reduced to 1 or $1\frac{1}{2}$ miles per hour; the maximum speed of a Mark IV (1917) was 3.7 m.p.h., of a Mark V (1918), 5 m.p.h., and of a "Whippet", 7 m.p.h. Partly because of this, but for other reasons too, they were extremely vulnerable. Out of 378 fighting tanks at Cambrai, 179 were hit on the first day, and only 92 remained by the fourth day. At Amiens, out of 415 fighting tanks in action on August 8th, only 145 were left on August 9th. Exploitation was ruled out, unless other Arms could do it; they could not.

'As to the generals, among those who (outside the Tank Corps itself) made good use of the new weapon in the British Army, we may list: Haig himself, a firm believer in them; Sir Ivor Maxse, who made possible their only success at Passchendaele; Sir Julian Byng, under whom they planned and fought Cambrai; Sir John Monash, who experimented boldly with them at Le Hamel; Sir Henry Rawlinson, who, after scepticism in 1916, gave them their best opportunities in 1918; and Sir Arthur Currie, who used them appreciatively at Amiens and against the Hindenburg Line. Neither Foch nor Ludendorff, however, seemed to be greatly impressed by them.'

It was, in fact, not until 1940 that the key appeared which could unlock the defensive barriers of the Western Front; and then the doors were flung wide open. That key was the technological advance which made possible the Blitzkrieg of modern tanks and aircraft. Even so, before the Second World War could be won by the Allies, an inexorable necessity remained; it was precisely as Haig had stated it during the previous war, on March 28th, 1915:

'We cannot hope to win until we have defeated the German Army.'

Once again it was found that, in order to achieve this end there would have to be 'Sommes', 'Passchendaeles' and 'Verduns'—only now they were called Orel, Kharkov, Leningrad, Moscow, Stalingrad. This time they did not take place on the Western Front, and they were not fought by the British; they were Russian victories, the foundation of Russia's power in the world today.

FRANZ SE METE EN PROBLEMAS DE AMOR

FRANZ SE METE EN PROBLEMAS DE AMOR

CHRISTINE NÖSTLINGER

Traducción de Juan José de Narváez

Ilustraciones de Erhard Dietl

GRUPO
EDITORIAL
norma

Barcelona, Bogotá, Buenos Aires, Caracas,
Guatemala, Lima, México, Miami, Panamá, Quito, San José,
San Juan, San Salvador, Santiago de Chile.

Título original en alemán:
LIEBESGESCHICHTEN VOM FRANZ,
de Christine Nöstlinger.
Una publicación de Verlag Friedrich Oetinger, GmbH, Hamburgo
Copyright © 1991 por Verlag Friedrich Oetinger, Hamburgo

Copyright © 1994 para Hispanoamérica y los Estados Unidos
por Editorial Norma S. A.
A.A. 53550, Bogotá, Colombia.

Primera reimpresión, 1995
Segunda reimpresión, 1996
Tercera reimpresión, 1996
Cuarta reimpresión, 1996
Quinta reimpresión, 1997
Sexta reimpresión, 1997
Séptima reimpresión, 1998
Octava reimpresión, 1998
Novena reimpresión, 1998
Impreso por Cargraphics S.A. — Imprelibros
Impreso en Colombia — Printed in Colombia
Septiembre, 1998

Dirección editorial, María del Mar Ravassa
Edición, Cristina Aparicio
Dirección de arte, Mónica Bothe

ISBN: 958-04-2697-X

CONTENIDO

Franz quería a muchas personas.

Quería a su padre y a su madre.

Quería a su abuela y a Josef,
su hermano mayor.

Quería a Gabi, que vivía
en la casa vecina.

Quería a Daniel Eberhard,
su compañero de escuela.

Y además, quería a sus tres tías.

Como la mamá, el papá, la abuela, Josef, Gabi, Daniel Eberhard y las tres tías también querían a Franz, él no tenía mayores problemas con el amor. Para Franz el amor era cuando dos personas se llevaban muy bien entre sí y se sentían muy contentas estando juntas (podían discutir un poco, pero sólo de vez en cuando).

ANA

Como Franz sólo conocía el amor fe-
liz, la tristeza de su hermano Josef lo
tenía desconsolado desde hacía unas
semanas. Josef se había enamorado de
Ana a primera vista. Él la había visto y
había sentido un vuelco en el corazón,
un escalofrío en la espalda, y se le había puesto la piel de gallina.

«¡Quiero a esta niña más que a nadie!», pensó Josef.

Josef se había encontrado con Ana
en el descansillo de la escalera. Mien-

tras él bajaba corriendo, ella subía de prisa y se estrellaron.

Ana llevaba un bolso debajo del brazo y se le cayó.

—¡Bobo, ten cuidado! —gritó.

—Discúlpame —le dijo Josef y recogió el bolso.

Ana le arrancó el bolso de la mano y siguió camino hacia el tercer piso. Josef permaneció inmóvil. Alcanzó a oír que la niña timbró en el apartamento de la señora Leidlich. Por cierto, la señora Leidlich no tenía un timbre común y corriente, sino uno que sonaba «ding-dong-ding-dong». Luego escuchó que la señora Leidlich le dijo:

—¡Ah, por fin llegaste, Ana!

Josef iba a casa de su amigo Otto, pero dio marcha atrás y regresó a su apartamento (porque el amor le había salido al encuentro en aquella mirada). Mamá y Franz estaban en la cocina. Lloraban un poco: mamá porque estaba cortando cebolla y Franz porque se encontraba muy cerca de mamá.

Josef se dejó caer en el banco de la cocina.

—¡Acaba de estallar! —dijo él.

—¿Dónde? —preguntó mamá, mientras trataba de contener las lágrimas.

—¡Dentro de mí! —contestó Josef, y les narró la historia de Ana, el vuelco en el corazón, el escalofrío, y les confesó que se le había puesto la piel de gallina.

—¡Tenía que pasar! —dijo mamá.

—¡Quiero volver a verla! —exclamó Josef.

—Entonces siéntate en la escalera y espera a que baje —le dijo mamá, sonriendo y secándose las lágrimas. No lo dijo en serio, pero Josef sí lo tomó en serio y se sentó en la escalera a esperar.

Debió soportar toda clase de comentarios de los vecinos:

—Siempre pierdes la llave de tu casa, ¿no? ¿Es que sólo tienes aserrín en la cabeza? —le dijo la señora Berger.

—Te pasaste de listo, ¿verdad? ¿Tu madre te dejó por fuera? —le preguntó el señor Huber.

—¡Tus padres han arrendado un apartamento, no una escalera! —gritó la señora Knitzwackel, que siempre lo regañaba.

Finalmente, después de una hora, Ana apareció en la escalera. Mientras la esperaba, Josef había pensado con detenimiento qué le diría. Escogió con cuidado estas palabras: «¡Me llamo Josef, vivo en este mismo edificio y me gustaría conocerte!» Pero antes de pronunciarlas debía carraspear para llamar su atención. Apenas había tenido tiempo de carraspear, cuando Ana pasó a toda velocidad junto a él. Josef saltó del escalón.

—¡Hola! —exclamó—. ¡Oye, espera!

—¡El «hola» murió hace mucho tiempo y el «oye» está muy enfermo! —le

respondió Ana desde el primer piso y luego sonó un portazo.

Josef regresó al apartamento y se encerró en su cuarto. Esto sólo lo hacía cuando estaba muy triste.

—Debemos ayudarlo —le dijo Franz a mamá.

—No sabría cómo —contestó mamá.

—¡Ya se te ocurrirá algo, si lo piensas bien! —añadió Franz.

Mamá lo pensó por un rato. Luego tomó una cesta con cerezas.

—Se las llevaré ahora mismo a la señora Leidlich y le diré que tenemos muchas y hay suficiente para todos —dijo mamá.

—¡Pero si no tenemos muchas! —gritó Franz. Él hubiera querido comer cerezas después de la cena.

—En todo caso, necesito alguna excusa para subir y hablar con ella —contestó mamá—. Así me contará algo sobre Ana.

Franz asintió y mamá subió al tercer piso con las cerezas. Allí permaneció

un largo rato y regresó con bastante
información.

Les dio las noticias durante la cena:
Ana tenía trece años, la misma edad de
Josef. Era sobrina de la señora Leidlich
y la visitaba todos los miércoles. Hoy
se había quedado más tiempo de lo
normal. Por lo general llegaba a las dos
de la tarde a tomar clase de piano y era
la señora Leidlich quien se la daba.

—¡Vaya, Josef! —intervino papá—. Entonces no hay razón para que te desesperes. ¡Cada miércoles tendrás una nueva oportunidad!

Desde aquel día, Josef se sentaba en la escalera cada miércoles faltando cinco minutos para las dos de la tarde y Ana pasaba dos veces junto a él.

Pero en el preciso instante en que Josef comenzaba a hablar, ella lo interrumpía con respuestas burlonas:

—¿Pretendes enfriar el río Po?

O bien:

—¿No tienes nada mejor para hacer que sentarte aquí?

Y en cierta ocasión la tía le dijo a Josef:

—¡Tú, el cómico idiota de la escalera, montando guardia de nuevo allí abajo!

Franz no entendía esto y pensaba: «Nuestro querido Josef es un muchacho maravilloso. Esta niña no pudo haber encontrado a alguien mejor».

—Estoy de acuerdo —opinaba mamá—. Pero para que se dé cuenta de ello debe empezar por conocerlo.

Cierta vez, un miércoles, Josef estaba resfriado. Tenía los ojos rojos y la nariz hinchada, y no quería que Ana lo viera. Abandonó su puesto en la escalera, se tendió en el sofá y miró a lo lejos. Franz pensó que había llegado el momento de actuar y buscó una excusa para subir al apartamento de la señora Liedlich. Mamá estaba en el trabajo y no podía ayudarle a encontrar la excusa, y esta vez no había cerezas. Entonces Franz tomó la cesta de papas, subió al tercer piso y timbró.

—Tenemos muchas ¡y hay para todos! —le dijo Franz en voz baja y le ofreció la cesta. (Cuando Franz estaba

nervioso siempre hablaba en voz baja.)

La señora Leidlich miró las papas sorprendida.

—Pero... ¿por qué? —balbuceó.

Franz le entregó la cesta con timidez.

—Bueno, pues reciban mis agradecimientos —murmuró la señora Leidlich.

En realidad, Franz debió haberse retirado en ese momento, pero no lo hizo. Se quedó allí, y como la señora Leidlich no quería cerrarle la puerta en la nariz, le preguntó si quería entrar.

Franz se asomó por la puerta y oyó que de un cuarto provenían las notas de un piano. Ana estaba sentada ante el piano y lo miraba con mala cara. La señora Leidlich suspiró.

—Tengo que enseñarle a tocar el piano, pero ella no quiere.

—¡Yo sí quiero! —mintió Franz.

—¡Siempre es así! —dijo Ana—. ¡Quien quiere, no puede, y quien no quiere, debe hacerlo!

—¿Me dejas probar una vez? —preguntó Franz.

Ana lo dejó sentarse ante el piano
con gusto. Franz echó una ojeada a la
partitura. No sabía leer las notas pero
vio que en el margen superior decía:
«EL PEQUEÑO HANS».

¡Por supuesto, él ya conocía esta can-
ción! Con el dedo índice tocó algunas
teclas y muy pronto, después de algu-
nos ensayos, encontró las notas ade-
cuadas.

—¡Pero si tienes talento natural!—exclamó encantada la señora Leidlich.

Le preguntó a Franz si quería tocar el piano con Ana, pues pensó que sería bueno para su sobrina.

—¡Claro que sí! —exclamó Franz.

En ese momento sonó el teléfono en el vestíbulo y la señora Leidlich corrió a contestar.

Mientras ella hablaba, Franz aprovechó para contarle a Ana que tenía un hermano mayor maravilloso. Que ganaba todos los premios en natación y en las carreras de esquí, y que era tan fuerte que podía pelear contra cuatro niños de su edad al mismo tiempo.

—Y cuando él no quiere hacer algo —añadió Franz—, ¡sencillamente no lo hace! ¡Nadie puede obligarlo!

En ese momento regresó la señora Leidlich y Franz dejó que le enseñara las notas musicales. Pero de vez en cuando contaba algo interesante sobre su hermano. Franz estuvo practicando las notas durante una hora entera. No lo hacía con mucho gusto, pero cuando la señora Leidlich lo invitó a que volviera el miércoles siguiente, él aceptó con alegría.

Franz no contó en su casa que ahora estaba estudiando piano, porque quería ayudarle a Josef en secreto. Durante toda la semana, Franz se rompió la cabeza tratando de encontrar la manera de subir a escondidas, el miércoles siguiente, al apartamento de la señora Leidlich. Josef ya se había curado de la gripe y por eso, ese miércoles montaría guardia en la escalera. Pero Franz se podía ahorrar esta preocupación porque ese día Josef no saldría del colegio a su casa, sino que asistiría a un partido de baloncesto. Franz llegó puntualmente al apartamento de la señora Leidlich. Practicó con Ana la escala de do mayor y la de sol mayor.

—Toma ejemplo del pequeño. Lo hace mucho mejor que tú —le dijo la señora Liedlich a Ana.

—Mi hermano mayor no dejaría que

tu tía te dijera eso —le murmuró Franz al oído de Ana.

Después de la clase de piano, Franz acompañó a Ana a su casa. Ella vivía a dos cuadras de allí. Durante el camino, Franz le habló de Josef. Exageró bastante pues en realidad él no era tan

valiente, ingenioso, fuerte e inteligente como Franz lo mostraba. ¡Pero esto causaba una gran impresión!

—¡Me daría mucho gusto conocer a tu hermano! —dijo Ana finalmente.

—¡Pero si ya lo conoces! —exclamó Franz—. Se sienta a menudo en la escalera porque le gusta reflexionar en silencio sobre los descubrimientos, la vida, el buen Dios, la justicia y otras cosas así.

—¡Y yo lo he llamado imbécil! —confesó Ana, arrepentida.

—Eso no importa —dijo Franz—. Ahora ya lo conoces mejor.

Franz regresó a casa muy satisfecho y encontró a Josef. Estaba sentado en el banco de la cocina.

—¡Acaba de estallar! —le dijo Josef.

—¿Dónde? —preguntó Franz.

—¡Dentro de mí! —contestó Josef.

Luego le contó a Franz que en el partido de baloncesto había visto a una niña lindísima. Había sentido un vuelco en el corazón, un escalofrío en la espalda y se le había puesto la piel de gallina. Le gustaba muchísimo; de eso estaba seguro.

—¡Quiero a esta niña más que a ninguna!

—¿Y Ana? —preguntó Franz en voz baja.

—Me decepcionó hace mucho tiempo —contestó Josef; y de eso también estaba muy seguro.

Desde entonces, Franz iba a su clase de piano cada miércoles. La señora Leidlich se hubiera enfermado si él hubiera dejado de ir. Además, Franz la había empezado a querer y no quería que se enfermara.

Por lo demás, Ana no volvió a la clase de piano los miércoles porque había convencido a su mamá de que no era justo obligar a alguien a aprender música.

Franz se encontró varias veces con Ana en la calle. Ella siempre le preguntaba por Josef y Franz se ponía de mal humor porque veía en sus ojos mucha nostalgia. Entonces hizo el firme propósito de no volver a entrometerse en los problemas de amor de los demás.

SANDRA

Estuvo bien que Franz hubiese decidido no preocuparse más por los enamoramientos de otras personas, puesto que muy pronto dejó de tener tiempo para hacerlo. Él mismo se encontró metido hasta las orejas en su propio problema de amor. Todo comenzó en la fiesta del cumpleaños de Gabi. Había muchos invitados y, naturalmente, Franz también estaba allí.

Franz no era un extraño, casi se podía decir que hacía parte de la familia de Gabi. Hacía un par de meses que almorzaba en la casa de ella casi todos los días, pues la empleada doméstica se había ido y su mamá estaba trabajando. A veces también iba a visitarla en las tardes e incluso el domingo. A menudo Franz y Gabi tenían sus pequeñas rencillas pero no permanecían enojados mucho tiempo.

En la fiesta estaba Sandra. Gabi se había hecho amiga de ella en el colegio hacía pocos días. Esto no le moles-

taba a Franz. Gabi estaba en otro curso y a él no le importaba con quién jugara en los recreos o con quién compartiera su merienda. Pero luego, en la fiesta, se sintió muy incómodo por esa amistad. Gabi y Sandra no dejaban de abrazarse, murmuraban, se sonreían con malicia y se tomaban de las manos. En cambio, para Franz, Gabi no tenía ni un minuto disponible. Cuando se despidieron, Sandra le dijo a Gabi que vendría a visitarla más a menudo.

—Conque ésas tenemos —murmuró Franz, pero Gabi no alcanzó a escucharlo. Estaba ocupada entregándole a Sandra un detalle de recuerdo de su fiesta.

Franz fue a quejarse con mamá.

—Toda niña necesita una amiguita. Eso es normal, querido Franz —le respondió.

Entonces fue a quejarse con papá.

—Gabi es muy variable. Verás que pronto se disgustará con Sandra —le contestó.

Franz tuvo confianza en las palabras de su padre y esperó a que se pelearan, pero no lo hicieron. ¡Todo lo contrario! Ahora encontraba a Sandra todos los días en casa de Gabi, y Franz pasó a un segundo plano.

Ellas conversaban alegremente acerca de camisas, pantalones y peinados, estrellas de cine, mascotas bonitas, esmaltes para las uñas y muchachos. Ensayaban bailes y escribían versos. A menudo se susurraban cosas al oído.

—¡Esto no es para ti! —le decían a Franz.

Sandra siempre quería jugar a la princesa y al príncipe. Ella hacía de príncipe y Gabi de princesa. Un día, cuando le propusieron a Franz que hiciera de bufón de la corte, él se enfadó; y cuando ellas le explicaron que no debía molestarse por eso, puesto que era muy pequeño para hacer de príncipe, Franz se puso rojo, le arrojó el gorro de bufón a Sandra y salió corriendo a su casa. Se tendió sobre la cama y le dio puños a la almohada, sollozando.

Así lo encontró Josef al regresar a casa. Le preguntó a Franz qué le pasa-

ba pero no le respondió. Él estaba esperando a mamá para contarle sus penas y, por lo tanto, Josef no podía consolarlo.

Pero esta vez mamá tampoco pudo ayudarle. No le parecía bien que le hubieran dejado a Franz el papel de bufón, pero no era para tanto. Y papá no se mostró nada comprensivo.

—Muchacho, no tienes por qué estar celoso de una niña. Si Sandra fuera un Sandro, podría entenderte —le dijo.

—¡Da lo mismo que se trate de Sandra o de Sandro! —respondió Franz.

—¡No! —exclamó papá—. ¿Acaso estoy celoso de las amigas de tu madre? Ellas no me van ni me vienen. Sólo me preocuparía si se tratara de un hombre.

—¡No me importa! —gritó Franz—. De todas maneras ya no quiero a Gabi.

—Sólo hasta mañana por la mañana —dijo Josef. Y esto lo irritó aún más.

Al día siguiente, Franz salió a las siete y media de su casa. Diez minutos después llegó Gabi, como todas las mañanas, y timbró con fuerza en casa de Franz. Si la señora Huber no le hubiera dicho que Franz ya había salido, probablemente hubiera seguido timbrando hasta las ocho.

Al mediodía, Gabi esperó a Franz a la salida del salón de clase, pero Franz salió con Daniel Eberhard y pasó de largo frente a Gabi, como si ella no existiera. Gabi quedó tan desconcertada, que lo siguió con la mirada atónita. Tampoco encontró a Franz a la hora del almuerzo. Él llegó con hambre a casa y entró en la cocina. La pared que separaba la cocina del apartamento de Gabi era tan delgada que se podía escuchar cuando hablaban en voz alta. Franz oyó a Gabi decir:

—Franz es un tonto. No sé por qué actúa de esa manera tan estúpida.

Luego la madre de Gabi entró en el apartamento de Franz y le sirvió un plato de arroz con verduras y una porción de torta de manzana. Ella tenía una llave del apartamento para casos de necesidad.

—¿Qué te pasa, Franz? —le preguntó.
«Ella debe saberlo, pues ha estado presente varias veces cuando su hija me ha ignorado», pensó Franz.

—¿Es por causa de Sandra? —le preguntó la mamá de Gabi. Franz comenzó a llorar y ella le prestó su pañuelo.

—Te comprendo, Franz —le dijo consolándolo. Franz sollozó y buscó refugio en su regazo. En ese momento decidió contarla entre la gente a quien él más quería.

—Pero si Gabi te quiere mucho —le dijo abrazándolo—. Créeme. Sencillamente ignora que te hace daño. Ella no ha sentido celos y por eso no los entiende.

«Si eso es así, yo le ayudaré a entenderlos. Le enseñaré lo que es sentir celos», pensó Franz. Comió a toda prisa y fue a ver a Gabi.

—¿Ya estás bien, Franz? —le preguntó Gabi.

—Más o menos —dijo Franz.

Gabi quería jugar con Franz a «ponte-el-sombrero».

—Esperemos a Sandra. ¡Quiero jugar con ella! —le dijo Franz.

—¡Pero si «ponte-el-sombrero» se puede jugar entre dos! —gritó Gabi.

—Bueno —replicó Franz—, pero con Sandra será mucho más divertido.

Al parecer, esto le molestó mucho a Gabi. Cuando Sandra llegó, Franz celebró alegremente su llegada; le elogió el vestido y el peinado; y luego le habló del osito de felpa que ella quería para su cumpleaños. Le preguntó si quería ir al cine con él o al menos a su apartamento. Su mamá había comprado un nuevo esmalte para las uñas, «rosado y muy elegante»; y también podría mostrarle una maravillosa antología de lindos versos.

Franz tomo a Sandra del brazo y Gabi se irritó aún más.

—Franz, todavía estoy aquí —le insinuó.

Franz no se dio por aludido. Se puso el gorrito y le dijo a Sandra que era la princesa más hermosa del mundo. Lue-

go hizo de bufón para ella: Dio volteretas, hizo muecas y contó chistes. Sandra se reventaba de la risa, y cada vez que Gabi pretendía jugar con ellos, Franz la detenía diciéndole:

—Hoy te toca hacer de príncipe, y hoy el príncipe está enfermo, así que quédate en la cama descansando.

Cuando Franz le susurró algo al oído a Sandra, Gabi se puso roja y le tiró la corona de príncipe a Franz.

—¡Váyanse a casa, los dos, ya! —vociferó Gabi.

—¿Qué le pasa a Gabi? —preguntó Sandra.

— Creo que ahora sabe lo que es sentir celos —le respondió Franz satisfecho y se fue a su apartamento silbando, ansioso por saber qué pasaría después.

Gabi lo visitó en la tarde.

—¡Oye, Franz! —le dijo—. Lo lamento de verdad. Durante los últimos días no he sido muy amable contigo.

—No le he dado importancia —le contestó Franz con indiferencia, sin dejarle ver su alegría.

—¿Quieres que no sea tan amiga de Sandra? —le preguntó Gabi.

—¿Harías eso por mí?

—¡Por ti, lo haría todo! —exclamó Gabi.

—No tienes que dejar de ser amiga de Sandra —repuso Franz—. Sólo tienes que repartir tu amor de manera más justa entre Sandra y yo.

—Pero así saldrías perdiendo —dijo Gabi—, porque en realidad yo te quiero a ti diez veces más que a ella.

Desde entonces a Franz no le molestó que Gabi y Sandra murmuraran entre ellas y hablaran de cosas que a él no le interesaban. Y una vez, cuando estuvo a punto de sentir celos otra vez, pensó en aquella tarde cuando Gabi le había declarado su amor, ¡diez veces más grande! Tampoco le puso atención a Josef cuando éste se rió irónicamente y le preguntó:

—¿Apostamos a que Gabi también le prometió a Sandra que su amor por ella era diez veces más grande?

—Yo no apuesto. Mamá siempre dice que apostar no es bueno —respondió Franz, tranquilamente.

ELSA

Las tres tías de Franz se llamaban Kitti, Kathi y Koko. No eran tías de verdad, las tres eran amigas de juventud de mamá. Vivían en un pueblo pequeño, en una casa con un enorme jardín. Ninguna de ellas se había casado y ninguna tenía hijos, pero a todas les gustaban los niños. Por eso, con frecuencia llamaban a la mamá de Franz y le decían que les gustaría tener al querido Franz con ellas por un par de días.

La tía Kitti era peluquera. La tía

Kathi era modista. Y la tía Koko era masajista. El salón de peluquería de la tía Kitti quedaba en el sótano de la casa. La modistería de la tía Kathi se hallaba en la mansarda. Y la tía Koko visitaba a sus clientes en automóvil. En el baúl llevaba la mesa portátil de masajes.

Desde hacía mucho tiempo Franz quería volver a visitar a sus tías y por fin pudo hacerlo en Semana Santa. El primer día, la tía Koko fue a recogerlo en el auto. Las tías no podían tomar vacaciones para cuidarlo, pero esto no le molestaba a Franz. Le gustaba mirar a la tía Kathi cuando cortaba y cosía. Incluso le podía ayudar a la tía Kitti en el salón de peluquería: Cuando ella le cortaba el cabello a una clienta, Franz barría el pelo del piso. También le hubiera gustado acompañar a la tía Koko a hacer masajes, pero ella le decía:

—Franz, no te puedo llevar conmigo porque mis clientes se tienen que desnudar para que yo les haga los masajes y no creo que les guste que tú estés ahí.

Además, Franz podía jugar en el jardín. Allí había árboles para trepar, tierra para cavar y un gato salvaje que se mostraba manso si lo llamaban con una salchicha.

En el jardín de los vecinos había una niña que se llamaba Elsa y parecía un duendecito. Sus ojos eran del color del cielo. Tenía el cabello largo y dorado, una naricita respingada y los más tiernos hoyuelos en las mejillas. Además era un poco más pequeña que Franz, lo cual era muy curioso, porque pare-

cía tener su misma edad y hasta entonces todos los niños de su edad eran al
menos un palmo más altos que él.

Franz se enamoró de Elsa tan rápido como Josef de Ana. Algo estalló dentro de él cuando la vio por primera vez
en el jardín vecino. El corazón le dio
un vuelco; pero no sintió escalofríos en
la espalda ni se le puso la piel de gallina. Al principio no se acercó a ella. Sim-

plemente la observaba desde la copa del cerezo, desde la ventana de la mansarda donde estaba la modistería y desde la claraboya de la peluquería. Elsa siempre parecía estar aburrida. Se paseaba de un lado del jardín al otro, arrancaba tallitos de hierba y flores, arrojaba piedrecitas y ensayaba a dar saltos largos.

Las tías notaron que Franz miraba a Elsa con interés y le advirtieron:

—Oye, Franz, la primera impresión

que da esa niña, engaña. Según dicen, es un pequeño diablo. ¡Cuídate de ella!

—Pero, ¿qué me puede hacer? —preguntó Franz.

—Puede seducirte —replicó la tía Kitti.

—¿Seducirme a hacer qué? —preguntó Franz.

—A hacer cosas malas —repuso la tía Kathi.

—¿Como cuáles? —insistió Franz.

—No podríamos decirte exactamente —respondió la tía Koko—. Pero todo el mundo murmura de ella.

Esto le pareció emocionante y llamativo a Franz. En ese momento sintió un escalofrío en la espalda. Ahora, sin lugar a dudas, tenía que conocer a Elsa. Se hizo peluquear por la tía Kitti para verse mayor y se echó a la boca un dulce de menta para evitar el mal aliento. Luego inhaló tres veces profundamente y salió al jardín. Elsa estaba recostada contra la cerca contemplando el cielo, como si estuviera observando un ave. Pero en el firmamento no había ni siquiera una nube. Franz se aproximó a la cerca. No quería hablar porque tenía miedo de que la voz se oyera sin fuerza, como le pasaba siempre que estaba nervioso.

—¡Vaya, por fin! —exclamó Elsa, sin dejar de mirar al cielo—. Ya estaba pensando que tenías algo en contra de las niñas.

Pero Franz no tenía nada en contra de ellas, así que negó con la cabeza.

—¿Eres mudo? —preguntó Elsa.

Dejó de contemplar el cielo y lo miró fijamente. Entonces a Franz se le puso la piel de gallina, como le había pasado a Josef. Nunca había visto unos ojos tan hermosos y tan azules.

—Dime que no eres mudo —insistió Elsa.

Franz negó de nuevo con la cabeza.

—Pásate a este lado —le propuso Elsa.

Franz saltó la cerca con mucha gracia y facilidad.

—¿Jugamos a algo? —le preguntó Elsa.

Franz asintió.

—¿A qué jugamos? —preguntó ella.

Franz se sentía ahora un poco menos nervioso y su voz se oyó casi normal cuando dijo:

—Cualquier cosa está bien, lo que tú quieras.

—¡Juguemos a algo prohibido! —dijo Elsa, y se le formaron dos hermosos hoyuelos en las mejillas. Franz reflexionó, pero no sabía de ningún juego prohibido.

—¿Qué te parece si jugamos al supermercado? —preguntó Elsa.

Franz estaba algo sorprendido y pensó: «Jugar al supermercado debe ser como jugar a hacer compras. Eso es como para niños pequeños y no está prohibido». En ese momento el corazón le volvió a latir con fuerza.

—Está bien —respondió con firmeza.

—Bueno, entonces vamos —contestó Elsa.

—¿A dónde? —preguntó Franz.

—¡Pues al supermercado! —exclamó Elsa.

Entonces Franz tuvo el presentimiento de que jugar al supermercado era algo distinto de jugar a hacer compras. Pero, temiendo que ella lo tomara por tonto, no preguntó.

—Iré rápidamente a informarle a mis tías que saldré al supermercado —dijo y trató de saltar nuevamente la cerca, pero Elsa lo sujetó por los pantalones.

—¿Bromeas? —gritó—. ¿Acaso también piensas llamar a la policía?

Tomó a Franz de la mano y marchó con él a través del jardín, calle abajo, hacia el supermercado. En la esquina se encontraron con un muchacho que miró a Elsa como si algo le hubiera estallado en su interior.

—Elsa, ¿puedo visitarte esta tarde? —le preguntó.

—No —le contestó Elsa, y señaló a Franz—. Ahora él es mi amigo.

Franz sintió un poco de lástima por

el muchacho, aunque se sonrojó lleno
de orgullo. En la esquina siguiente,
antes del supermercado, se encontraron con otro chico. Éste también miró
a Elsa como si le hubiera estallado algo
en su corazón.

—Elsa, ¿puedo ir con ustedes? —le
preguntó.

—No —le contestó ella, y señaló a
Franz—. Ahora él es mi amigo.

A Franz le brillaron los ojos de orgullo.

Pronto llegaron frente al supermercado y Elsa se apoyó contra un auto
estacionado.

—Ahora entra y tráeme una goma de mascar —le dijo a Franz.

—Lo lamento, pero no tengo dinero —repuso Franz.

—No tienes que comprarla, sino traérmela —dijo Elsa.

—¿Traértela? —susurró Franz. Ahora entendía cuál era el juego del supermercado. ¡Debía robar la goma de mascar!

Elsa miró su reloj de pulsera, que tenía segundero.

—Voy a medir el tiempo. Harold lo hace en tres minutos. Déjame ver si eres más rápido que él —le dijo.

Fue tal la sorpresa de Franz que no pudo decir ni una sola palabra. No quería robar, pero tampoco deseaba decírselo a Elsa. Ella le dio un empujón y Franz fue a parar a la entrada del supermercado.

«Dios mío, ¿qué voy a hacer ahora?», se preguntó.

Y justo cuando Franz abrió la puerta, recordó que en el bolsillo de atrás del pantalón tenía un paquete de cinco gomas de mascar, sin abrir. Esto le quitó un peso de encima. Corrió por el supermercado, dio la vuelta a la primera estantería, pasó delante de la cajera, salió de nuevo y regresó a donde lo esperaba Elsa. Sacó del bolsillo el paquete de gomas de mascar y se lo entregó.

—¡Maravilloso! —exclamó Elsa—. ¡Un minuto y diez segundos! ¡Eres el más rápido!

Lo miró llena de admiración y Franz se sintió el mejor de todos. Entonces llegaron los dos muchachos con quienes se habían encontrado antes y Elsa les contó la gran rapidez con que Franz lo había hecho. Ahora Franz se sentía un poco mejor que el mejor. Estaba tan orgulloso y ocupado explicándole a Elsa y al otro muchacho que para tamaña pequeñez, un minuto y diez segundos era demasiado tiempo, que no se dió cuenta de que uno de los muchachos había entrado en el supermercado.

—Donde vivo, lo haría en cincuenta segundos —presumió Franz.

Entonces el muchacho salió del supermercado acompañado por una empleada grande y corpulenta, y ambos se lanzaron sobre Franz.

La empleada tomó a Franz por los hombros y lo sacudió.

—¡Es increíble! —gritó—. ¡Parece un ángel pero roba como un cuervo! ¡Dame la goma de mascar!

Elsa miró a la vendedora inocentemente con sus ojitos celestes.

—¡Oh, esto es terrible! —susurró Elsa y le entregó a la vendedora el paquete de cinco gomas de mascar—. En verdad no sabía que las hubiera robado. ¡Palabra de honor! Pensé que las había comprado.

La mujer tomó el paquete, lo examinó, sacudió la cabeza furiosa y soltó a Franz.

—¿Qué broma es esta? —preguntó—. ¡Este paquete no es de nuestro supermercado! ¡Nosotros no vendemos esta marca! —dijo, le entregó el paquete a Elsa y regresó al supermercado.

—¡Eres un bobo! —le dijo uno de los muchachos a Franz.

—¡Maravilloso amigo te has conseguido! —le dijo irónicamente el otro muchacho a Elsa.

—¡Eres un imbécil! —le gritó Elsa a

Franz, y le ofreció la mano derecha a uno de los muchachos y la izquierda al otro.

—Ahora me voy con ustedes. ¡Pueden acompañarme! —les dijo, y se alejaron saltando.

Franz los miró irse. Sintió un vuelco en el corazón, un escalofrío en la espalda y se le puso la piel de gallina. Pero de manera diferente de lo que había sentido antes. Ahora se sentía terriblemente enfermo.

Permaneció largo tiempo en el mismo sitio y luego regresó lentamente a casa de sus tías. No quería verlas, así que se coló por el jardín y se trepó a lo alto del manzano. En el jardín vecino estaban Elsa y sus amigos.

—No se pueden dividir cinco gomas de mascar entre tres personas. Así que dos son para ustedes y yo me quedo con tres —les dijo Elsa a los muchachos, y Franz la escuchó.

Al atardecer, Franz le escribió una carta a Gabi:

Querida Gabi:
La casa de mis tías es muy agradable
pero sin ti no estoy contento. Aquí no
hay niños con quienes jugar. Sólo hay
un duende en el jardín vecino, pero es
muy malo.

Tu Franz

Seis grandes lágrimas cayeron sobre
el papel mientras Franz escribía. Allí
donde caían, la tinta de color azul os-

curo se corría produciendo nubes de color azul celeste.

Cuando el cartero le entregó la carta a Gabi, Franz ya había regresado. Gabi corrió a verlo con la carta en la mano.

—¿La escribiste cuando estaba lloviendo? —le preguntó a Franz señalando las nubecitas de color azul celeste.

Franz las miró y sintió subir los colores a su rostro.

—¡Ah, sí! —murmuró—. Ese día hacía un tiempo horrible, pero muy pronto pasó —le dijo a Gabi con una sonrisa.